The Secret Keepers

The Secret Keepers: Narratives Exploring the Inter and Transgenerational Effects of Childhood Sexual Abuse and Violence

By

Susan Dale

CAMBRIDGE SCHOLARS

PUBLISHING

The Secret Keepers:
Narratives Exploring the Inter and Transgenerational Effects of Childhood Sexual Abuse and Violence,
by Susan Dale

This book first published 2013

Cambridge Scholars Publishing

12 Back Chapman Street, Newcastle upon Tyne, NE6 2XX, UK

British Library Cataloguing in Publication Data
A catalogue record for this book is available from the British Library

ISBN (10): 1-4438-4415-2, ISBN (13): 978-1-4438-4415-4

This book is dedicated to the memory of my wonderful mother Nell, and to my amazing children Adam, Sam and Becky who continue to inspire, love and support me in more ways than they know.

TABLE OF CONTENTS

ACKNOWLEDGEMENTS

Without the all of the contributor's courage and commitment this book would never have been born. There are not the words to adequately thank them, or acknowledge their part in the process, but I am hoping that they feel my unwavering respect and thanks. I also hope that people reading and standing alongside their words will gain inspiration.

Thank you also to:

- All my long suffering friends, colleagues and supervisees who have read and commented on the many drafts of the book without complaint.

- All the people I have worked with, who I have since lost contact with, but who have entrusted their stories to my keeping. Stories that have influenced and inspired me in the writing of this book.

- My wonderful supervisor Jan who as ever has "been there".

- My husband John who has again checked spellings and grammar and maintained my cabin in the garden such that it has become a haven to write in.

INTRODUCTION

Working as a therapist for nearly two decades, I have heard many stories from people who have experienced the effects of trauma as a result of childhood sexual abuse and violence, and also stories from others who have not been directly abused, but have somehow inherited from a parent, or even grandparent, effect from this kind of trauma. As my own mother was subjected to sexual abuse as a child these issues are very close to my heart. I witnessed firsthand the effects this history had on her, myself, and other family members, and when the opportunity arose decided to try to find ways of telling these, often silenced stories, in ways that empowered, and released the tellers, from what Joy, one of the contributors, describes as, "secrets that bind us to something so evil it can never be spoken of".

Keeping the abuse secret within families, seems core to the effect the trauma has on the lives of the families involved. As Gardener states: "The particular characteristic is that it is a transmission that takes place silently in secret, but actively (Gardener 1999:297); it is within this silence that the trauma disables those from leading what they would consider to be normal lives.

Childhood sexual abuse and violence often has a profound impact on the adult survivors and unless they are able to find ways of living with, and through, their experiences this will impact on how they live their lives and are able to relate to significant others; including their children. It seems important, therefore, within any research methodology to find ways of breaking the bonds of these silences in ways that empower those affected. Although the research project documented within this book was not undertaken with the express intention of being "therapy" my hope always was that it would prove therapeutic for those participating and that it would not only add to the body of research literature relating to childhood sexual abuse and violence, but also enable contributors to narrate their stories in ways that enabled them to develop a voice and find richer more coherent stories to live by. The study, I feel, overtly crosses the boundaries between narrative research and narrative therapy holding on to the ethical framework of both (Bond 2000, 2004).

The transmission of trauma across generations was first explored in depth within the psychological field by Freud (Strachey 1953-1976) and the impact early life experiences and relationships have on the thoughts, feelings, behaviours and relationships of people as they develop into adults is now well documented. (Mower 1962; Etherington 2008; Jacobs 1998). There has also been considerable literature written about how the trauma of conflict and war affects secondary generations (Schwab 2010; Virag 1984; Duba 1995) and also a growing literature base regarding the trauma of childhood sexual abuse (Etherington 2000; Alexander 1992; Browne and Finkelhor 1986), the effects of domestic violence (Wolfe et al. 2003; Kolbo, Blakely, and Englemann 1996) and even in the vicarious transmission of trauma to those supporting survivors (Jenkins 2002; Scauben and Frazier 1995). Within the last decade there has been a positive movement encouraging those affected by childhood abuse to speak out about their experiences; and a stream of memoirs and life stories have emerged such as (Pelzier 2002). Little however has been written about the intergenerational aspects of childhood abuse from the personal perspectives of the families affected.

Sometimes the second (or third) generations have no, or little knowledge about the facts of the traumatising events, but the effect, in terms of physical, emotional and psychological responses such as hyper-arousal, intrusive thoughts, terror, relational difficulties and despair are to use Schwab's phrase "haunting legacies" (2010:1). As Schwab goes on to point out "the transmission of violent legacies by far exceeds the passing on of historical knowledge or even of stories with thick descriptions of personal involvement" (ibid:1). People often report feeling, "traumatised, yet I don't know what by" (Excerpt from conversation with Joy).

The focus of the book is to enable people affected by inter, and transgenerational, aspects of trauma to develop a voice and explore ways of moving away from, "these secrets that cannot be told" (Patrick). It is not intended to be a learned thesis on trauma, sexual abuse or violence, but hopefully through the telling of personal narratives, and reflection on literature, some understanding of these issues will emerge.

The seventeen contributors come from a wide background of experience and age. Some have worked with me in the past in the context of consulting with me in therapeutic settings, others have contacted me in my role as a researcher wanting to undertake narrative co - research

(Epston 2004), two came as a result of my advertising for participants in a professional counselling journal. They come from a wide range of age and life experiences; all have in common the experience of growing up with a parent, or with the history of a parent, who had been traumatised. All our writing is collaborative, and to the best of my abilities, what the contributor's want to say about their lives, which interestingly is not necessarily what I would have thought to ask about. They have all made choices about whether they wish to write anonymously, or to write under their own names. Most have chosen to use pseudonyms which they have chosen. All have read the final manuscript before publication, and most have chosen to comment on their experience of being involved within this project and the research.

My doctorate and subsequent research projects (Dale 2010, 2011) have all used narrative and life story methodologies to work collaboratively with people in ways that enable them to co-research their experiences and find a voice. My practice as a therapist is also influenced by narrative practices where identity is seen as something socially constructed within relationships and the stories people tell of their lives. It is with these ideas in mind I approached this project. Within qualitative research it is often the researcher's voice and choices that predominate. I tried to enter the project with an open mind, and to respond with a process suitable for the stories engaged with; rather than with set ideas about what we should talk, or write, about. I did have some ideas about narrative practices that may be useful, and some thoughts on intergenerational and transgenerational trauma; these were, I hope, offered tentatively as ways forward rather than directives. I have tried to make the process of research as transparent as possible; in order to enable the participants to have a good understanding of what they are embarking on, and you the reader to travel with us on the journey.

To summarise, this book demonstrates a dynamic research process in action, which hopefully offers the reader an insight into the lives of a group of people affected by inter and transgenerational trauma, and continues my exploration of the therapeutic, and research uses of narrative methodologies It is set out in Four Parts:

Part 1 Keeping it in the family explores through the stories of Liz, Alex, Joy, Duncan, Matthew and Jason; the effect of childhood sexual abuse and domestic violence on the family and includes commentary relating to

current literature relating to domestic violence, sexual abuse and intergenerational trauma.
Part 2 Spiritual and Religious Settings explores through the stories of Helen, Joanne, Patrick, Elsa and Anne, the effect of sexual abuse and violence perpetrated within spiritual settings, has had on the lives of the following generations. It includes a commentary exploring current literature relating to abuse within the church and initiatives set up to support families affected.

Part 3 Conflict and War explores through the stories of Sajela and Orthie, a sister and brother, their experiences of being the caught up in a country torn by war and cultural conflict. It includes a commentary relating to inter and transgenerational trauma caused by war, and brief background literature relating to the conflict in the Democratic Republic of Congo (where Sajela and Orthie originate).

Part 4 Breaking the Bonds of Secrecy documents the research process and includes both a commentary, and a demonstration, of a "definitional ceremony", and "collective biography", in action. Contributors then reflect on the research process. The focus here is to exploring the use of narrative practices (both research and therapy) as a process of transformation.

Terminology

I have used the terms counselling, therapy, and psychotherapy interchangeably to mean a therapeutic undertaking agreed upon by someone who is commonly called a client and someone who is called counsellor, therapist, or psychotherapist.

The term intergenerational trauma I have taken to mean trauma that is directly passed down from one generation to another. Transgenerational trauma has been used to describe trauma that can pass across several generations.

Narrative Text

As with other writing (Dale 2010, 2011) where conversation has been turned into text; the text is presented in stanza format in order to more accurately represent the spoken word. The spoken word after all is as Tedlock (1983) points out more akin to poetry than to prose. The line breaks, capitalization, and spaces represent the pauses and emphasis put on particular words and phrases. It is a format used by other social science researchers and interested readers can find fuller descriptions and explanations in the work of Richardson (1990; 2003), Etherington (2000) and Speedy (2005).

PART I

KEEPING IT IN THE FAMILY

CHAPTER ONE

CHILDHOOD SEXUAL ABUSE AND THE FAMILY

> "When someone does that to you; someone who ought to be looking after you, it messes with your head. They tell you to be "daddy's special girl" and because you need loving, you do, and you hate it, yet crave the being special. I have never talked about what happened then. It was my problem. The shame of it, the terror of it, has affected everything in my life. When I left home, what I did as a job, who I married, the way I looked after my kids. It affected everything." (Liz)

Sexual Abuse

I met with Liz (quoted above) back in 1991 when I had just started doing some informal counselling for a local charity. At that time I had just completed a basic training in counselling, and had only limited academic training in childhood development, and the traumatic effects of abuse. I did however have a lot of personal experience of the effects of childhood sexual abuse. I had grown up with a mother who had extensive knowledge of these matters, and who shared a lot of her experiences and wisdom with me. Liz was 79 at the time of our conversations and had been talking to me about her long association with mental health problems. I felt, and still feel, sad that she and many other people who are sexually abused have never been able to talk about what happened to them. It is sobering to realise that in 1937 when Liz was growing up, childhood sexual abuse was not considered by many professional academics in the psychological fields as traumatic, but rather an acting out, by the child, of inappropriate sexuality. It was referred to by Bender and Blau as "sexual delinquency" (Bender and Blau 1937:511). To those of us working with survivors of childhood abuse in 2012 this may seem a totally crazy interpretation, but it is our cultural history, and an attitude that we have inherited that even to this day colludes with the silencing acts of sexual abuse.

Herman writes that, "traumatic events call into question basic human relationships. They breach attachments of family, friendship, love and community. They shatter the construction of the self that is formed and sustained in relation to others (Herman 1992:51; Etherington 2008:25). It is therefore unsurprising that people who have been traumatised by childhood sexual abuse, and who have not been able to address this trauma, bring to adulthood many unresolved issues which then have to be negotiated within personal relationships and parenthood. Whilst some of these negotiations are successful, with people finding extraordinary ways of re-authoring their lives outside abuse, for others the journey is a much harder one that profoundly affects both the person and those they are in relationship with.

Next follows an exploration of research literature which has been drawn together to gain some kind of understanding of the impact childhood abuse has had on adult survivors. This does not mean that everyone who has been sexually abused will have experienced all of these issues, but most I feel will be able to identify with at least some of the following.

What is Trauma?

The Encarta English dictionary describes trauma as, "an extremely distressing experience that causes severe emotional shock and may have long-lasting psychological effects". When we are subjected to situations that shock us, or challenge everything we thought to be safe or true about life, or our lives, we need the resilience (Skodol 2010) and opportunity to find strategies to incorporate this new knowledge in ways that enable us to continue to live out our life. For example; a young woman recently consulted me in relation to an incident that had happened at her place of work which she had found particularly traumatic. She had been present during an armed raid in the shop where she worked. This event had challenged everything she had thought to be true about the safety of her neighbourhood, and her beliefs about people. When she was able to develop new ways of thinking that integrated these new experiences into her life (this involved re-evaluating her beliefs about the nature of people and taking some steps within her workplace to ensure her safety) she then felt "very different. This was now just one of the things that had happened in my life; a historic event, rather than an ongoing drama that I was stuck in". When a person is confronted however with multiple traumas or a trauma so challenging, or not spoken about, it is often difficult to integrate this into existing life experiences. The emotional repercussions of the trauma then continue to remain active in the present and can affect many aspects of the person's existence.

Research confirms that children are usually deeply traumatised by sexual abuse (Brown and Finkelhor 1986; Putman 2002), and that this trauma is often not spoken about (Salter 1995; Etherington 2000), or integrated, meaning that the effects are felt through into adulthood. As Sinason asks, "what happens when the toxic nature of what is poured into the undeveloped vulnerable brain of a small child is so poisonous that it is too much to manage?" (Sinason 2002:4). This is not to say that children (or survivors) do not have strategies to cope. Children can be extremely resourceful when confronted with the trauma of sexual abuse. Alex describes how as a child he was fearful that sexual abuse would destroy him:

> "I was deeply traumatised; everything that should have been safe suddenly became unsafe. I had no control over anything. I wasn't sure if I could go on living with this and I knew I had to gain control over something if I was to survive. Although I was a child, I knew it was a life or death struggle. That is why I started thinking about dying, and suicide, and planning my own death. I could control whether I chose to live or die and this gave me hope I think".

Liz describes how she coped with the trauma of abuse as a young child:

> "I used to pretend to be someone else when it happened. Never Liz. Liz was separate from the abuse. That happened to another girl, she was different from me in every way. She was small, I was tall; she was dirty, I was clean; she had bad manners, I was good. She felt things, I never felt. Without her I wouldn't have survived at all. Most of the time I completely blocked her out from my life, I just went to school and got on with life. Because I needed my mother and father I also took on their voice. I could shout at 'her' to and that felt good actually, and I could still love them".

These kinds of coping strategies as a response to trauma are amazingly effective for the child, but are not generally sustainable in the longer term because they interfere with our ability to grow and develop in relation to other people and the world around us. As Sinason points out of the kind of splitting of self that Liz describes, "it is a brilliant survival mechanism when facing the trauma of abuse, but it is maladaptive when the trauma is over" (Sinason 2002:8). We are left, as Alex and Liz were, with "the strategies of survival becoming the problem" (Liz). For Alex this meant suicidal thoughts and behaviours threatening his life[1] when he encountered further trauma as an adult, and for Liz, the splitting of herself into three

[1] To read more of Alex's story see Dale (2011)

distinct personas fragmented her sense of self and her ability to feel and to relate to others resulting in broken relationships, and a mental health diagnosis.

Linking childhood abuse with PTSD

Post traumatic stress disorder (PTSD) is a relatively new title for the kind of reactions to trauma that have been around since the beginning of recorded time. For example Samuel Pepys kept a diary of his reaction to the Great Fire of London in 1666 which include a description of his own nightmares some six months after the event (Salter 1995; Daly 1983). It has been called in the past anything from "hysteria" to "shell shock". It occurs when a traumatic memory cannot be processed and placed as a historic event in the person's life. The trauma and the feelings, thoughts, and behaviours that this elicits remain active in the person's present day life. So the person remains in a constant state of alert, poised it would seem for "fight or flight". There is a recurrent cycle of intrusive thoughts, images and feelings followed by periods of emotional numbness (Salter 1995). Flashbacks, nightmares, feelings of intense distress and even physical reactions (such as pounding heart, shortness of breath, nausea and even paralysis) often occur when the person is reminded of the event (MIND 2011). People affected constantly relive the experience of the past event in the present; causing extreme distress and an inability to engage in life going on around them.

Research has been undertaken (Rothschild 2000) showing how trauma affects the brain, and demonstrates that there is a physiological change in people who have been subjected to trauma and develop PTSD. There is also evidence that this physiological change can be transmitted through the generations. Yehuda et al. (2005) conducted a study of pregnant women who developed PTSD after being indirect witnesses of the terror attack on the World Trade Centre in New York on September 11th 2001. It was shown that the mothers and their babies both had abnormally low levels of cortisol, which in turn can lead to the development of stress led conditions and health problems associated with regulation of the immune system (Etherington 2008:45).

Not everyone who is exposed to trauma goes on to develop PTSD (Bonanno 2004) or have the same responses to the trauma (Terr 1991). Over the last twenty years there has been considerable debate as to whether PTSD is an inevitable outcome of childhood sexual abuse, or whether it is just one of many different outcomes. For example studies by Herman (1992) and Kendall-Tacket (2000) imply that PTSD is universal within groups of people sexually abused as children, whilst studies by Resnick et al (1993) Greenwald and Leitenberg (1990) showed only a proportion of people who have been sexually abused as children were affected by PTSD symptoms; although the Greenwald and Leitenberg study did show evidence that participants had been affected at some time in their life. As Salter points out however, "there are a number of symptoms associated with child sexual abuse that cannot be subsumed under the current definition of PTSD" (Salter 1995:195). These she goes on to list as a high risk of mental health problems, suicide, drug addiction, alcoholism and re-victimization. Before turning to literature relating to these issues let us first turn to questions of attachment, and how the fragmenting of relationship with our principle carers can effect how we develop as adults.

Attachment theories and childhood trauma

The idea that the relationship a child has with his or her parents, or major care provider, has a huge impact on how that child grows up and develops as an adult has come to underpin most psychological theories. Bowlby's studies undertaken in the 1940's and 1950's noted that, "babies formed a strong bond with their primary caregivers, which if broken, caused children great upset and distress" (Howe et al. 1999:12) and he went on to purport that when this bond was disrupted it caused great impact on the child's development and the subsequent patterns of attachment and how the adult formed relationships. (Bowlby 1988).

It has been shown that children who have loving caring attachment figures can demonstrate resilience when faced with trauma (Etherington 2008; Cloitre, Morin, and Linares 2004) they are more able to ask for support from those around them and find the inner resources to soothe themselves (Etherington 2008). Childhood sexual abuse often disrupts these secure attachment patterns causing the child to be traumatised by the abuse and also where the perpetrator is the principal care giver, results in the lack of a secure attachment figure. This is traumatic for the child, and often traumatic for the adult looking back at what happened to their child selves. The abuse does not necessarily have to be physically violent to be experienced as traumatic. Often in the case of childhood sexual abuse the abuse is not physically violent; many perpetrators using psychological manipulation rather than violence to obtain their sexual gratification. This kind of manipulation however, has a devastating impact on the development of trust, which forms the basis of relationships and how the person sees themselves. As Etherington points out:

> "When those who inflict injury are people upon whom the child depends, the impact on the child's development of trust is severely damaged. The closer the relationship between the child and those who betray them, the greater rupture in their ability to bond with others and form secure attachments" (Etherington 2008:41).

Salter describes the impact of the perpetrator on the person abused as leaving, "footprints in their mind" (Salter 1995:3). If someone is or has been physically violent towards you then the footprints left are very evident and clearly delineated as being made by another. If the abuse however is couched in words of love and care then the footprints are much more difficult to distinguish and erase. As Liz states:

> "There was this part of me that believed – still believes I was to blame. Not him. If I start to think about what happened.... it is always shame and then blame heaped on me. Even though, logically now I know it was not my fault. I still have thoughts like that deeply ingrained as part of me."

Liz talks about the negative thoughts that she has about herself as being "deeply ingrained" within her sense of self, and confirms that they have become part of her identity.

Identity Issues

Identity however, is one of those slippery terms that seem easy to define, especially when we are thinking of someone else, but incredibly difficult when it comes to defining who we are. When we ask the question, "what it does it mean to be me?" we come across all sorts of complications and a reluctance to be fitted within the parameters of a specific label. There are various theories as to how identity or personality are formed these being mainly related to the thorny debate on "nature or nurture". Are the answers to who we are written into our genetic make up, or are they due to our upbringing and the experiences of our life? I guess that I have come over the years to believe that it is probably a mixture of both. After all there are some things in our genetic make up, over which we have no control over. For example I was born with a visual impairment, and this is part of who I am and how I identify myself, and something I have no ability to change. Also as discussed previously, our experience of early attachment does affect how we relate to others and this also has a huge bearing on how we identify ourselves. We can and do internalise other people's opinions of us; these can, and do, become part of how we identify ourselves; this can be negative or positive. I am however much more comfortable with the notion of identity being something that is socially constructed through our relationships with others and the stories we tell about our lives. This gives us much more flexibility in changing how we view ourselves, and indeed how others view us. Using the example I used earlier of my visual impairment. I cannot change the physiology of my condition, but I can and do constantly re-author (White 2007; White and Epston 1990) and renegotiate my relationship with visual impairment. This in turn changes my thoughts and feelings about being visually impaired and also other people's reaction to my disability. If I am confident and non-defensive about my visual impairment then, I have found, the other person is more likely to respond in a positive way.

Having the freedom in this way to change how we identify ourselves makes a huge difference to how we live our lives. In the case of sexual abuse, those abused can find themselves totally defined by their abuse as either, "victim" or, "survivor". Being stuck within the confines of either of these labels is not always very helpful. As Alex points out:

> "One of the reasons I was reluctant to talk about my experiences of sexual abuse was that I would be labelled as a "victim" with all the expectations from Jo public that might have. I didn't want to be a "victim" neither did I want to be a "survivor" with the hero label that I could never live up to. I am just me. A person. Bad things happened to me, but to be defined by them would mean giving them more credit than they deserve and also eat up all the good things that I also am. "

Mental and physical health

There have been clear links between childhood sexual abuse and the development of mental health problems in adulthood (Mullen et al. 1993) and also in dependence on drugs or alcohol (Ravandal et al. 2001; Felitti et al. 1998; Etherington 2008). Etherington (2008) points out that workers in the substance misuse field have often recognised that addiction problems often link with childhood sexual abuse issues, and she points to a study by Rohsenhow et al. (1988) who found that two in three substance-abusing women, and around two in five men said they had been sexually abused as children (Etherington 2008:46) which is an extraordinarily high figure. A large study (over 17,000 participants) conducted by Dube et al (2005) also confirms the link between childhood sexual abuse, substance misuse and mental health and other social problems and highlights the prevalence of childhood sexual abuse amongst adult populations.

Although childhood sexual abuse is not the only cause of mental health issues such as depression, acute anxiety, PTSD, bi-polar or dissociative disorders, it has been shown that many people who have been sexually abused as children do have a higher risk of developing these conditions than those in the population who have not been affected by childhood sexual abuse issues (Mullen et al. 1993). High rates of suicide and self-harming behaviours are also linked to childhood sexual abuse (Browne and Finkelhor 1986; Winter et al. 2009).

Having looked at some of the literature relating to mental health and childhood sexual abuse, it is perhaps important to note that there is also a growing body of evidence showing that unprocessed trauma can also lead to a person developing psychosomatic disorders and as Etherington points out, "a range of diseases that are known to have an autoimmune component such as arthritis and heart disease; and certain endocrine problems such as thyroid dysfunction" (Etherington 2008:47).

Studies also show the link between childhood sexual abuse and different patterns of sexual relationships Noll et al point out:

> "Abused participants were more preoccupied with sex, younger at first voluntary intercourse, more likely to have been teen mothers, and endorsed lower birth control efficacy than comparison participants. When psychological functioning earlier in development was examined, sexual preoccupation was predicted by anxiety, sexual aversion was predicted by childhood sexual behavior problems, and sexual ambivalence" (Noll, Trickett, and Putman 2003:575).

To summarise, not everyone who has been sexually abused as a child will develop problems in later life, but it would seem that research shows childhood sexual abuse can affect a person's mental and physical health, affect how they identify themselves, their sexuality, drug and alcohol use and how they relate to others, and that these effect can sometimes be felt throughout their lives (Itzin 2006).

Intergenerational aspects of Childhood Sexual Abuse

If our parents, or grandparents, have lived through the trauma of childhood sexual abuse, what does that mean for us; the following generations? If we go back to what has been said about attachment and the importance the relationship a child has with his, or her, principal care giver; it would seem fairly clear that if a person who has been traumatised goes on to develop longer term mental and physical health issues arising from the trauma, this may have implications for the way in which they are able to relate to their children. This is not to say that all those effects are necessarily negative. From a personal perspective for example I can see clearly how my mother's early experiences enabled her to strive always to keep her children (and grandchildren) safe from abuse. How she was able to love deeply and without judgement. She always taught me that to be judgemental of another was the worst possible crime. "I know" she said. "People have judged me, but they can never know the whole story and what happened". She was a good listener; because being listened to was something she would have liked for herself. As I grew up, people were often to be found sitting round our dining table with a cup of tea talking about a crisis. She was fearless and stubborn, "if you put your mind to it, it can be done. I have survived too much to let this beat me" were mantra's she encouraged us all to live with.

There were however negatives outside of her control. Her mental health, the trauma of what had happened infecting our daily lives. Fear and flashbacks threaded their way across the generation gap. As Liz explains:

> "When I had my children I was determined that they would not have the experiences I had had. I suppose in some ways I was totally extreme in my protection, wouldn't dream of letting them go anywhere out of my control and of course they did, and just didn't tell me! I started to get very strong OCD[2] symptoms when they were small children and it was a nightmare even going shopping. I had to check on them and do all manner of things just to get myself through the tills. Sometimes I would have flashbacks in the house. My daughter remembers distinctly being about 4 or 5 and being dragged behind the sofa by me and silenced when someone knocked on the door. She started having nightmares and being afraid of the dark. I blamed myself of course".

---

[2] Obsessive Compulsive Disorder

In recent years there has been interest in the secondary or vicarious transmission of trauma, for example where professionals working with survivors of traumatic events go on to develop the symptoms of post traumatic stress (Etherington 2000:145) so it would seem appropriate to surmise that children who are subjected to accounts of their parents trauma will also be likely to be traumatised.

Studies carried out looking at the intergenerational aspects of trauma (mainly in response to the families of holocaust survivors) but also in respect of the children of service personnel who have had diagnosis of PTSD (Dekel and Goldblatt 2008) show clearly that the thoughts feelings and behaviours of a parent in relationship to trauma do influence the effect on the child. Dekel and Goldblatt examining literature relating to armed service veterans involved in conflict and the transmission of trauma to their children note:

> "Fathers with PTSD have difficulty containing their emotions, and their attempts to mitigate pain lead to a massive use of projection mechanisms, where severe emotions such as persecution, aggression, shame and guilt are split and projected onto their children. As a result the children may identify with the projected parts of their fathers' emotions, and perceive his experience and feelings as their own" (Dekel and Goldblatt 2008:284).

There is also literature emerging which shows the likelihood of PTSD being transmitted genetically (O'Brian 2004) and not just as a response to a traumatic event, or a learned behaviour. The Australian Institute of Health and Welfare (2004) showed that the children of Vietnamese military veterans were more than three times as likely to commit suicide than the average Australian population. This ties in with the findings from other studies carried out mainly in response to secondary generations of the holocaust (Segman et al. 2002). Not coming from a background of medical or genetic research this is not an area that I feel able to comment on, but as you will see through later chapters; the contributor's experience is often of the symptoms of trauma without the knowledge of the event.

CHAPTER TWO

JOY

Joy was referred for counselling in 2009 by an agency that I work for from time to time. This particular agency offers support to employees (including counselling) who work for local government. Joy had requested counselling because she was feeling particularly anxious about her daughter's childcare and this was impinging on her ability to work. She felt that her anxiety was linked inextricably with the things that happened to her as she was growing up so we used our sessions together to talk about these issues. We decided to record our sessions together (so that she could take the recordings home and listen to) and I also kept notes which I emailed to Joy between sessions for her to reflect on. This is the story of our work together and I hope demonstrates the use of narrative therapy practices within a brief counselling intervention.

Joy – Counselling Sessions 2009

I grew up with secrets,
I knew how to keep them from a very early age
big ones and small ones.

I was always amazed when I went to friends houses
and they talked about all sorts of things
just sitting round the dinner table.
Everything seemed to be on the table and
somehow..
transparent.
Whether it was where they were going,
who they liked didn't like
what they felt about stuff.

In my house nothing was ever talked
about
except on a one to one level
with the knowledge
you should never tell

Sue: Journal May 2009

I met with a young woman today who talked about her skills of "keeping secrets" and how this was inherited from her mother who had been sexually abused.

I recognise the skills I think that I inherited a similar legacy. I also realise that her experiences will be unique and not my own. I perhaps need to reflect on my own experiences to ensure I do not identify with her in a way that interferes with the therapeutic process.

other members of the family…
Even really basic stuff that shouldn't be a secret ..
I'll give you an example:
When I started having driving lessons I found out the cost;
£15 a lesson.
My mum agreed to fund them,
but only if I didn't tell my dad or brother.
She always kept her personal finances very close to her chest. She and my dad did not have a joint account or anything.
We were not hard up, my dad had a good job
but she did not want him to know.
So, I always had to stand at the end of the road to meet my driving instructor.
When I had been having lessons for about a year I took my test and passed.
Then came the problem – what was I supposed to say to dad and my brother?
So I just blurted it out..
Why didn't you tell us said Dad.

We could have helped you with the cost!
He gave me a cheque for £200
I just felt guilty, guilty, guilty.
Mum just kept quiet.

This is just a silly example,
The secrets were about all sorts of stuff
that really
didn't need to be secret.
Whether it was
a major trauma
(like my brother getting involved with a gang)
or buying sweets at the local shop
all of it was treated like some kind of big secret.

When mum was diagnosed with breast cancer she didn't tell anyone.
Not even my dad.
She had chemo…
her hair fell out.
Dad who was beside himself with worry
(because she was so ill)
eventually forced her to tell..
but she hated him knowing
and us knowing.

Session notes June 2009

As we talked today I was amazed by how strong you were when your mum was ill. You were such a small child then. You described yourself as, "a champion coper" and I think you were just that, and perhaps this is a skill you still find uses for today?

Even though you went along with what you see now as, "all that crazy-ness" you did what you could to support both your mum and your dad. The fact that they did not talk to each other was something you as a child of 8 could do nothing about.

As a child,
you just go along with it.
It is only as an adult looking back that it sounds really crazy.
It also seemed infectious.
I kept secrets from her,
my brother kept secrets from me.
Somehow there was this big wall of ice forming between us all.
We could see each other moving about during the day,
eat together, talked together,
but there was this frigid space between us that could not be broken through.

Mum also was paranoid about my safety.
She would see danger in everything.
I wasn't allowed to use a bicycle,
or roller skates.
As for going on a school trip or taking music lessons…
It was always,
"but what if something happens?"
I felt sometimes that she wrapped me up in cotton wool that suffocated.

Session notes July 2009

You talked about, "the big wall of ice" that was between you all. What was that like I wondered? I had assumed that it was a difficult thing but you told me that although the ice kept you separate from each other it was also "beautiful" because it also gave you the, "freedom to be who you wanted to be without having that judged by the others in your family".

We looked also at the "infectious nature" of secrets, and how as well as giving freedom they also meant that you couldn't support each other as a family.

I became really not confident in myself or my abilities
I think that still is there really,
even now.
If anyone asks me to do something I haven't done before
I always think, "you won't be able to cope with that".

It made the world a very scary and impossible place.
When I was 18 and went off to university I was terrified
that I wouldn't cope,
that I would die crossing the road
or that I would stop breathing in the night
and no-one would find me
I really, really struggled.
My friends didn't understand at all how going to a festival or a gig could totally paralyse me with fear.

The GP put me on anti-depressants because he thought that university was causing depression,
but looking back I don't think I was depressed
I was just coming from a dysfunctional family

I had just had an abortion, and I was coming into an environment
where there wasn't this ice between people
and it was really scary to start talking to people about my feelings and fears;
most of these fears were totally irrational.

What helped a lot was going to see the university counsellor.
She really helped me understand all of what was going on in terms of how my parents were.

The other thing that was a real problem was sex.
Mum didn't talk to me at all about sex, or relationships.
If I asked she would say,
"you're only a child, enjoy your childhood".
I wasn't allowed to wear make up,
or clothes that made me look older.

Sue: Journal July2009

Talking to Joy has made me think more about my family's ability to keep secrets and whether there were any benefits for me growing up in that kind of atmosphere. In the past I have only ever thought about it in a negative light, but talking to Joy I have begun to wonder whether there were any benefits for me. The word that comes into mind is freedom. Not having to tell people everything about you means that you can be whoever you want to be. In my case it felt at times as if I lived in two worlds. The world of my parents, eating, sleeping and talking about trivial things, school and this other world where I could do anything I wanted – providing I didn't tell! I wasn't wicked or rebellious. They thought of me as a quiet musical girl with a few friends, whereas I had boyfriends, went to parties got drunk and stayed out too late. Although this sounds like normal teenage behaviour, it did feel different, whereas my friends would do these things and feel guilty about keeping things from their parents, I felt no remorse. This was a separate life they didn't have to know about. This gave me quite a lot of power, but also a lot of responsibility because I couldn't share the important decisions with anyone and my own knowledge of life was limited by lack of years. I was also so afraid of anything and everything and couldn't ask for parental reassurance.

I learnt the facts of life from school sex education,
and then Mum came to the school and complained!
As a teenager ..
I don't know whether it was a throw back from all this protection
I became quite promiscuous.
Took ridiculous risks
and of course eventually ended up pregnant.
when I was 17 – just before university.

I eventually talked to my dad

and he took me to a clinic…
where I had a termination.
I still have nightmares about that.
That baby..
I wish….

I just fell apart.

Dad must have plucked up the
courage to talk to mum about it.
because out of the blue she started
to tell me everything.
She didn't talk about **me** or the
abortion
But everything about her life.
I mean **everything**
about her life as a child,
the abuse,
what happened to her as a child.

Too much information on top of
what I was going through really.
What I didn't realise at the time
was that she had never told
anyone else about what had
happened
not even Dad.
I didn't realise he didn't know
until…

There was a TV programme on
about sexual abuse which really
upset mum,
I said to Dad something like:
"I expect it brought up really
difficult memories".
He was really shocked.
I never found out if he talked to
her about it.
Mum kept talking to me though.
Over and over about what had
happened,
how she had felt…
It was one of the reasons I
gathered the courage to leave
home.

Session Notes Sept 2009

You talked today about going to a clinic with your dad to have a termination, and how difficult this was for you. I wondered what this was like for you going through all of this without being able to talk to your mum. You assured me however that in this kind of situation it was your dad who you relied on. His "steadfastness" was what got you through things whereas your mum's reactions were often extreme and usually focussed on her.

You went on to tell me about other instances when your dad's "steadfastness" had held you, and enabled you to feel safe. I asked you if noticed any of these qualities anywhere else; you spoke of your relationship with your daughter and how, whatever else happens, you try to be steadfast in your love for her.

Session notes October 2009

We talked a lot today about sexual abuse and how the, "not talking about it" and then how the, "talking about it in graphic detail" were both really hard for you. You spoke of needed to be: "an expert juggler" to try to negotiate the balance between listening to one of your parents without betraying the confidence of the other. I was really impressed at how long you managed to do this, and how it must have helped your Mum to be listened to.

Leaving home was a good decision, which enabled you to engage with others and be "a real part of something".

I know it probably sounds incredibly cruel,
but, I just couldn't bear her talking about it any more.

When I came back from my first term at university
things were back to normal.
The ice had reformed;
nothing was ever said again;
not for years and years anyway.

She had been abused by her father (my granddad) for years.
He had seen it as his right to have sex with all the girls
once their periods had started.
My mum had three sisters

Her mother (my grandmother)
had known about the abuse – how could she not?
Sometimes when the girls screamed at night because of what he was doing she would cry out, "leave those girls alone you bastard".
But that was it.
They never told anyone.
One of the girls got pregnant;
the child was passed off as granny's menopause baby.
I knew him as my Uncle Jack.
He had two children one of them a year or two older than me.
Did he know? I have no idea.

I asked her once why she had not told anyone.
"Who would I tell?" she asked;
well- the police, your teacher, your mother, your aunt!
"If they believed us my father would have gone to prison" she said.
"That would have left us all alone and destitute.
I don't think Mother would have coped
and then what would
have happened to us?
There were no social
workers around then
who would help".

I didn't know how to
respond to that….

I think that what
happened to my Mum
had an effect on
all of her life.
If it hadn't happened…

Session Notes Nov 2009

We talked for a long time today about the reasons your mother did not tell anyone about the abuse, and how you felt about that. You said that initially you felt really angry about it, but as you have got older then you realised that it is sometimes really difficult for people to make the "right" decisions because they are, as you said, "so tied up with the trauma of it all they can't think". You said that you were still very angry with your grandfather, and that even though he was now dead, you would never forgive him. We talked about forgiveness and what it would mean to forgive him. You felt that it would be, "a betrayal of everything I believe in".

Perhaps she would have been a different kind of Mum.

Saying that makes me feel very guilty,
she couldn't help what happened
and she did love me.
I guess she dealt with it in whatever way she could.
It did have a huge impact on me though.

Session Notes December 2009

Today we talked about sexuality and how your Mum's reaction to abuse had somehow affected your own sexuality and made you, "hyper-vigilant to my daughter". You thought this was something to do with the fact that she never talked to you directly about sex at all, and also perhaps about not being able to "model relationships". You talked about how the "ice" between you meant that you couldn't talk to her about relationships, or what they might entail, so you had to judge for yourself, and how this meant that you followed what other people wanted from you. Then having heard your Mum's story you then decided the only safe way of relating was in a non-sexual way. Even now that still affects how you relate to men. You want your daughter to have a different experience, but are not sure how to achieve this as yet. One of the things that really struck me was when you said, "every time ice crystals form between us I use an imaginary blow torch to blast them out of the way. This means that we can talk to each other." You did wonder however whether at some point she would need to keep some secrets from you and how you would manage that when she got older.

She was a kind of "smother mother";
that made me want to push away from her;
which is where the guilt comes in, I think.

I didn't have the right kind of boundaries around sex.
I either didn't have any sexual encounters at all with anyone
(even my husband)
or I was promiscuous having sex with anyone without thought.
It seemed to have a different meaning for me.

When we had Lucy….
I could feel in myself
my Mum's fear
I was scared
to leave her alone
with **anyone**.

All the time I was eyeing up strangers thinking

"is he going to abuse my daughter"
It was driving me mad.

I could see also the damage that
kind of thinking had done to me
so I fought against it.
Surprise, surprise I ended up
divorced.
I don't blame Kevin.
It must have been hell
living with me.
I wouldn't even trust his dad.

Also on the sex front,
one minute I was
all over him,
the next
the frigid ice maiden!

We get on alright now,
we only have contact when she
goes to stay.
Strangely he is the one person I do trust with her.
I did share with him what had happened to my mum…
I remember - he was so shocked and appalled
and amazed even that I trusted him with my daughter.
And I do..
I think.

Most of the time…..

My GP thought at one stage I had bi-polar disorder
I did go and see a psychiatrist for an assessment,
but he said he thought I really wasn't bad enough
for them to help.
I kind of minimised what I said to him though!
He suggested different anti-depressants.
I picked up the prescription
but I never took them..

I guess being part of the "system" seems too scary.

They might say I am mad,
in which case they would lock me up
and throw away the key.
Then what would happen to my daughter?

Session notes Dec 2009

I wondered, as we were talking, what it said about you and your values that you are so concerned about whether strangers are going to abuse your daughter? You told me that one of your core principles was to, "have the kind of love for children that puts them first rather than my needs". You went on to explain that this was at times tricky; but that you were proud to have managed to achieve this; part of this was to trust even your ex-partner, because even though you didn't like him, you trusted him not to abuse your daughter.

I hear myself echoing my Mum.

Perhaps that is how she felt?

Knowing something is wrong,
but fearing….
So much fear.

The remedy might be;
even worse than the sickness.

The other thing that happened when my daughter was born,
I started thinking about my biological father…

I know I have always talked about dad
as if he were..
but,
around the time when I was a teenager
I had to send my birth certificate off to get my driving licence,
I noticed that it said on it: "father unknown".

Mum of course wouldn't speak about it,
Dad however said that Mum was pregnant when he first knew her.
He didn't know who my father was,
but just felt that because he was there when I was born he was my dad.
I agreed with him.
This actually felt ok at the time.
After I had Lucy however,
I thought about it more and more…
Eventually I confronted Mum.
What I learnt shocked me so much….
and it is so hard to talk to Mum…

Session notes December 2009

You talked to me today about what your mum told you about who your biological father was. This seems HUGE, but somehow not what you have thought important to talk about. I wondered why this might be. You told me that it was firstly about your loyalty to your dad, and how you loved him, and also what was said felt so surreal that it was difficult to connect to, and so shocking to look at the implications that you had shut it out. I asked whether it was something you wanted to explore now and we looked at ways we could possibly do this. You thought that my idea of writing it all down might help, then we could perhaps talk about it.

Unsaid words to my mother
Joy

The day you told me who my father was
the world stopped.
I stopped.
Like a physical blow
chopped across my life.
Until then
on my birth certificate,
"father unknown".
I asked for answers.
The answer however
stopped me in my tracks.
Shocked me beyond belief.
This changed everything,
everyone,
I felt fractured,
broken,

Unclean.
Taunted by something beyond my control.
"The secret".

Questions echo through my mind:
what about my child?
What does this mean for my daughter?
Your granddaughter.

How did it happen?
Why did you not tell me?
I feel sick,
sick to the stomach.

What about granny?
Dad, my brother?
What about my Uncle Jack?
Did they know about me?
Who I was?
How am I related to them all?

When grandpa was alive you used to take us to visit.
I remember loving to sit on grandpa's knee,
and

YOU
YOU let me.

I feel sick again.

How could you put me in such danger?
Was it to protect your secret?
Was the secret more important than your daughter?

I feel so angry.
Raging in fact.

A pain cuts across my chest.
Just who am I?
Who are you?
Am I a genetic monster?

HOW COULD YOU GET AWAY WITH HAVING YOUR FATHER'S CHILD?
The second in a family.

Things become clearer;
make more sense now.
When I was 12 and my periods started
You were consumed with grief;
And you tried to keep me a little girl.

Now I guess that this is about
when you became a "little woman".
It started then.

You talked to me once
about the abuse;
but not about having me.
What did you do when you found you were pregnant?
What it was like carrying your father's child?
I wish you could talk to me.
An avalanche of words comes from you
but no eye contact,
no answers,
just shame.

I noticed the next time we meet
you have cut your arms again.
So I let it go,
but in the letting go is the silence of the secret.

Can I live with this secret?

How can I love you so much
yet hate what has happened.
The need to know, to find someone
anyone
to blame.

I look at my daughter
so perfect,
so beautiful,

Could I talk to her about this one day.
I'm not sure.
Will she feel she has the right to know too?

I am who I am.
She will have the ability to be whoever she wants to be.
Perhaps genetics are just that:
genes;
not responsible for how we live our lives.

Session Notes January 2010:

It was our last session today – we have had 6 monthly meetings which you have said have been helpful in that you now understand the connections between what happened to you as a child, and what is going on for you now as a mother. From my perspective they have helped me understand something of the intergenerational effects of sexual abuse.

You thought it may be helpful for us to list some of the achievements over the months and your goals for the future, which are also enclosed.

A summing up of our work together:

Achievements (in your own words):

- *A closer more accepting relationship with my mum.*
- *A letting go of the negative stories about who I am.*
- *A melting of the icebergs that surround me and distance me from people.*
- *Having the confidence and the ability to judge who is a safe person to leave my daughter with.*
- *A letting go of the, "anxiety who swallows all the good out of the world and who I do not have to have a close relationship with".*

What you think are important goals:

- *You want to ensure your daughter grows up able to talk to you about things that concern her, but also to remember that she needs some private space too.*
- *To keep your daughter safe, but to remember that although there are some bad people out there in the world, not every man is a paedophile.*
- *To carry on learning to as you put it: "love myself and not be too judgmental of who I am".*
- *To tell yourself stories of hope as opposed to just concentrating on the stories of "pain and failure"*

As I write all of this down I am amazed by all you have achieved and just know that you are as you put it "on the right track". We decided not to meet again at the moment, but you know that we can in the future, if this is something that you would like.

Over the following years I have occasionally met up with Joy, and she has emailed me to let me know how she is getting on. In the Autumn of 2011 we met and discussed the possibility of writing something about our work together. She had been reading one of my books and has been really interested in how people tell stories of their situations which help others.

We talked about privacy, and whether she wanted to write in her own name. She decided after careful thought to adopt a pseudonym to protect the identity of her family, and people who would be exposed by her writing and could not give their permissions. She thought she would like to include the above excerpts from our conversations, and also write a short story that somehow encapsulated her experiences of being a mother and a daughter "caught in the web" of sexual abuse. She was also very interested in my journal excerpts from this time as she had not realised my mother had also been sexually abused. She felt that this was probably the reason I had understood so clearly what it had been like for her growing up. As she said, "your situation was different, but it did give you a window through which you could see me".

Joy: Caught in a Spider's Web

Once upon a time in a far northern country there was an evil, malevolent spider. He lived in the corner of a deep dark cave. The cave was very cold. Ice crystals formed on the huge web that he spread over the entrance. He was always looking for a mate. His taste was for the young and the innocent. He lured them into the cave by playing sweet music on his ice flute, and when they came to sit by his feet to listen they became entangled in his web and could not escape.

Immobilised they became his ornaments and play things and he kept them there until the light of knowing appeared in their eyes. Then he cast them out, sure in the knowledge that others would come to him who were still young and innocent.

The young and innocent ran skipping back into the warmth of their countries, so glad to be free. Although they were free, wrapped around their bodies were strands from the web glittering with shards of ice. This meant that try as they might, getting close to others was very difficult. Anyone they embraced was likely to be cut to ribbons, or risk hypothermia. The ice also insulated against sound, so however hot the day, and however much they craved music and speech or even love, they remained cold, silent and alone. Those beside them, even those they wanted to love, were alone and had to fend for themselves.

The spider still lives in his deep dark cave, unaware and uncaring about the web he has spread into the world, now he is just a spirit, his mates however have learnt the art of passing on the ice and the legacy goes on. Gradually the land around those he touched is freezing the only hope is for the courage of a new generation to bring the Spring.

CHAPTER THREE

DOMESTIC VIOLENCE AND THE FAMILY

> "One of my earliest memories, I must have been about 7, is of coming down into the kitchen and my father had my mother pinned to the floor with his foot across her throat, she was just making gurgling noises. I remember being paralysed. Like a rabbit in the headlights. I didn't know what to do, how to stop this. Whether to go in and try to stop him or whether to creep out and pretend I had not seen? As I stood there he turned and saw me. Instantly he moved and I cowered away expecting that he would hit me. He didn't though; he just seemed to come back to himself. Carefully he moved away from my mother who lay absolutely still on the floor and tried to hug me. I struggled away from him and ran to the bathroom where I was sick. It was a process that over the years repeated with different levels of damage being inflicted to both my mother and the house. Within a day or two however things would be back to normal and he would be; just the same jolly loving Dad he always was. It was like he, and we as a family, had this double life. When I left home to go to university it was never spoken of again. It always kind of shocked me when I saw him with his solicitor friends being totally charming and the model of gentleness, that there was this other side that was never talked about".

Eva talks about her early childhood memories of how domestic violence intruded on her life. She says she feels that the visual memories of these events, "are imprinted in my mind". Even though her father never physically assaulted her, "quite the opposite really, he was always the really gentle dad towards me" the events were so shocking and traumatising that she feels they are affecting her as an adult, and her ability to have relationships. Eva comes referred by one of the employment assistance programmes that I work for. We talk about some of the reasons she feels are relevant to her current difficulties.

> "I guess that because I couldn't protect my Mum, and this whole thing about him being so violently angry. Sometimes he completely lost control; yet it was cloaked under this really loving way. This is the reason, I think, that I am so mistrustful of how men are. I cannot really believe it when

> they are; loving towards me. To protect myself I kind of push them away. I cannot trust what I see. I know that is experienced by the one I am pushing away as really hurtful; and it hurts me too, but I cannot seem to stop myself. Every time things start to go well, and I feel happy, then I do something crazy like flirt with other men then refuse to have sex with them. Say awful things. I know it is crazy, but I cannot seem to stop myself. Sometimes it seems easier to have relationships with complete bastards; because at least then you know where you are, and if you hurt them, then it is probably what they deserve."

There seems no doubt that if a child witnesses domestic violence, even if that violence is not directed towards them, they report experiences of trauma (Levendosky et al. 2002; Edleson 1999; Kitzmann et al. 2003). The Kitzmann et al. review of literature examined 118 studies showing a significant link between children being exposed to domestic violence and childhood psychological problems. Interestingly they found little difference in the outcomes between children who witnessed abuse, and those children who had actually been physically abused.

A study conducted by Ehrensaft et al. (2003)conducted a project following 543 children over a twenty year period to:

> "Test the independent effects of parenting, exposure to domestic violence between parents, maltreatment, adolescent disruptive behavior disorders, and emerging adult substance abuse disorders, on the risk of violence to and from an adult partner" (Ehrensaft, Cohen, Brown, Smailes, Chen, Henian et al. 2003:741).

The findings showed that childhood exposure to domestic violence conferred the greatest risk of receiving partner violence. There was also a correlation between childhood exposure to domestic violence and subsequent substance abuse disorders and what they describe as "conduct disorders" (ibid:742).

There is also some evidence (Stith et al. 2004) that witnessing violence in childhood has links with perpetrating or receiving violence in adult relationships, although the evidence is in my opinion somewhat insubstantial within this particular study. Other reviews such as the review of literature conducted by Holt, Buckley and Whelan show evidence that "Children and young people may be significantly affected by living with domestic violence, and the impact can endure even after measures have been taken to secure their safety" (Holt, Buckley, and Whelan 2008:797). They also point out that there is rarely a direct causal pathway resulting in a particular outcome, they see individual resilience, timely and individually tailored interventions and other social factors as influencing longer term outcomes.

So what does all of this research mean? I guess there are no real surprises for those of us who work with adults, who as children witnessed domestic violence, who like Eva, on the surface are fine, but deep down feel deeply traumatised. In earlier chapters when looking at the effects of childhood sexual abuse I used Salter's words, that the abuse left "footprints on the mind of the survivor" (Salter 1995:3) to describe the impact of sexual abuse. I consider that witnessing domestic violence also leaves footprints on the mind. When a young child experiences violence especially between the two people who they rely on for existence, the world becomes a very unsafe place and they need to find ways of adapting their behaviour to survive. Eva's story shows just how terrifying it can be to find yourself witnessing such violence, and then the violence not being spoken of or congruent with the person's normal demeanour. Her way of coping when she was small was, "not to trust anyone who was nice, that way I would never be lulled into a false sense of security". On the whole, this worked well for her as a child, and did indeed protect her. "I was the only one in the class not taken in by the crazy guy who used to try to buy the girls ice creams so he could feel them up". As an adult however, trying to form lasting relationships, deeper than friendship, she has found that it got in the way. "I'm alright at the chatty level, and the going out level, even the sex level, but if people want intimacy. If they want me to share something of myself, or trust them, then it feels like I'm going to die and I react badly".

As early as the 1940's and 1950's Bowlby was starting to notice the relationships infants had to their primary care givers and the difficulties for the child when something disturbed these relationships (Bowlby 1951, 1944). As How et al. point out, "children had to believe that their attachment figure was available psychologically as well as physically" (Howe et al. 1999:13) otherwise they developed adaptive behaviours to enable them to get closer. These broadly fall into three types: signalling behaviours; which encourage interaction with the mother or principal care giver, these could be looking appealing, or being good. Aversive behaviours such as crying, screaming, which are intended to stop the parent doing whatever it is that the infant finds intolerable, or send out signals of distress, such that the adult responds. Active behaviours that take the child towards the parent, such as crawling towards them when they are small, or actively seeking out close relationships with others (Belsky and Cassidy 1994). These behaviour patterns, unless we change them, become the patterns we keep using, even into our adult relationships. What does this mean for children who have grown up with their main care givers being subjected to violence.

Eva says:

> "I learnt very early on that I had to be good, I tried so hard to be the best girl possible for my mum. Otherwise I just got sort of side tracked. She was so afraid of my father. In private she rewarded me for being, 'my little angel'. I was devastated that I couldn't keep her safe from him though. I kind of thought; I should have been able to. With my father I tried to appease him all the time, and used to cry and snivel a lot, be really needy."

We talk about how these kind of patterns have affected her relationships as an adult. She tells me:

> "I think towards men I have always been very needy and clingy. This most of them seem to find a terrible turn off. I can hear myself sometimes on the phone begging for attention and I just know it is just so unattractive, but there I am doing it, and because I always choose such bastards they revel in it. Enjoy my squirming."

Changing these patterns was one of the goals for our work together, as was working to lessen the intrusive memories and trauma caused by witnessing such violence. As shown in the research cited above, often trauma symptoms are as apparent in witnesses to violence as those who are subjected to violence.

I was interested recently to speak with Jill a worker at a national project supporting women who are subjected to domestic violence, and listened to her thoughts on how children are affected:

> Jill: I suppose I know when I see the woman turn up with their small children, that this is not just about them, but it is also about those children.
>
> Sue: Can you say a bit more about that?
>
> Jill: The woman, is often totally traumatised. Quite often women physically shake when the phone rings, not quite believing that they are safe. There are a lot of feelings flying around. Anger, fear and sadness. There is not much room for the children. To start with, many of them are

either silent and clingy or outrageously behaved; tearing the place apart at every opportunity.

Sue: Does that change over time do you think?

Jill: Yes. A little, usually the quiet ones stay quiet, and because they are not causing much trouble they do not get referred on to other services, the ones with behavioural issues however are often referred on to specialist children services and often that helps with their behaviour.
The quiet ones bother me though. It is sometimes as if they want to be invisible….

I was thinking here of one particular little girl, she was about 3, still in nappies, and never uttered a sound during the 7 weeks she stayed at the hostel. Her mother managed to get housing elsewhere and they moved on, she had some counselling I think, but that little girl's face will stay with me for ever. I often wondered whether she would ever recover.

Sue: Do people ever come to you more than once?

Jill: Yes. Sometimes, many times. There is often a cycle where they try again, and then have to leave, and then come back. We try to encourage them, but it is hard I think to always let go of the fear and walk away.

I have been there so long now that I had a sixteen year old turn up a few months ago, who remembered me from when she was four and had come with her mum. She said "at least I knew where you were, and that you would keep me safe". I'm not sure that was a good thing or not.

Sometimes it is very depressing. Other times when people do move on it feels like a real "yes" moment.

The following chapter looks at my work with two brothers, also witnesses to domestic violence, and follows their therapeutic journey into what they describe as "wellness".

CHAPTER FOUR

CONVERSATIONS WITH DUNCAN AND MATTHEW

Duncan and Matthew are brothers. Duncan contacted me in 2004 following a referral from his GP for counselling. He told me that depression had been affecting him for over ten years and he had recently attempted suicide by taking an overdose of paracetemols. His brother Matthew however had visited unexpectedly and finding him unconscious had called an ambulance. Following a short spell in hospital he recovered physically and decided to try to address some of the issues he felt were, "at the heart of my depression". These were connected with, "the violence at home I witnessed as a child. Things I've never felt able to talk about".

What follows in this chapter are excerpts from my original conversations with Duncan (taken from transcripts of our counselling sessions in 2004 and retained by Duncan, and some of the emails I wrote to him between our counselling sessions). There then follows excerpts from the research conversations and writing with Duncan and Matthew completed during the course of 2010/11.

I have acted as editor, but all writing has been collaboratively constructed with Duncan and Matthew having the final say about what is included or excluded. Their names and some identifying information have been changed to protect their privacy and to ensure their families anonymity.

Conversations with Duncan May 2004

Commonly those people who approach a counsellor or therapist for support start by telling, "problem saturated descriptions"(Payne 2000:10) which only describe their life experiences in terms of the difficulties they encounter and what they have been unable to do. Although it would seem important to listen carefully to, and respect the pain and difficulty of the situations people find themselves in, it is also helpful to listen for alternative stories emerging that give hope and reflect strengths which the person can then use to circumnavigate their current difficulties. Alongside having conversations, one of the tools that narrative therapists often use to capture the achievements of individuals are what are described by Morgan as "therapeutic documents" (Morgan 2000:22). As Freedman and Combs go on to say these are important, "because there are multiple possibilities, infinite strands of experience and countless ways of interpreting any idea or event, important intentions and even accomplishments can get lost" (Freedman and Combs 1996:222).

Producing a document can bear witness to aspects of a person's life that has been neglected or forgotten. Within my work with Duncan I often used email documents to summarize some of what we talked about. Duncan also kept a journal and he and his brother Matthew wrote a number of therapeutic documents and letters some of which are include here which bore witness to their relationship and the stories they wanted now to live by.

Email from Sue to Duncan May 2004

Dear Duncan,

It was so good to meet with you last week.

One of the things that really struck me about our conversation was how important your family is to you. How even when you felt really desperate, you tried very hard to think about how you could protect them. You said that this kind of, "being the protector" was a role that you had taken on even when you were just a small child and you saw how frightened your brother Matthew was of your various step-fathers. You also told me of the steps you took to try to protect your mother, even though she found it very hard to go along with your ideas.

This protector role is one you have carried on into your own family where you have tried very hard to, "be a guardian angel" to your own children and have tried to treat your partner Elizabeth with respect.

You spoke of how this had all fallen apart when you had a "bloody row" with Elizabeth. You noticed a red mark on your son's back (he has just turned two) and she admitted hitting him. You describe how rage filled you "I just saw red... I wanted to kill her". You described how frightening this was and how appalled you were by these feelings thinking that you were turning into, "one of the men my mum lived with". It was this that made you decide that suicide was the best option.

One thing that really surprised me was that despite your close relationship with your brother Matthew, you have never talked with him about what it was like growing up alongside violence, and he has never talked to you about it either. I guess I am also curious to know what it was like for you growing up witnessing all this violence and trying to be the "protector". Perhaps this is something that would interest you to talk about when we meet next week, unless of course you think that there is something more relevant; you know better than me what kind of conversations would make a difference.

Conversations May – Sept 2004

Sue: I'm wondering what this was like growing up with this…

D: I guess it was the normal.
Just what happened in our family.
I didn't think about it when it wasn't happening;
the violence I mean.
I just blocked it out.
When it was happening there was just the terror.
This is what I wrote last week in my journal:

Small (me);
impotent (me),
couldn't stop (him),
hate (him),
fear (him),
dread (him),
ashamed (me).

shrouded in a cupboard;
the two of us,
my brother, and me.
Covering my ears to crush out the sound
of her screaming,
again, and again.

Then the silencing sound;
thump against flesh;
flesh against wall.

I wished I was anything but male.
I was ashamed of my sex,

I didn't want to grow up as a monster.

That's when it started, I suppose;
the trying to be feminine.
I didn't want to grow up as a monster.

Sue: As I listen to all of this I am amazed that you survived…
What got you through those times do you think?

D: I guess a couple of things really…
Firstly having my Nan close by.
I used to sit with her and she talked about stuff;
how her husband (my grandfather) used to beat her up
when he was drunk.
Because she was old, and ok,
it gave me hope that perhaps my mum would survive.

The other thing that helped was
pretending myself into a different life..

I used to pretend that I was a girl
and could chat with friends about nails, and hair,
and giggle a lot.
I joined, as a teenager, a couple of web sites using false names;
those hours were such a relief.
I was normal.

Sue: I'm wondering….
Would it be helpful to talk more about your Nan?
Or about the pretending….or something else.

D: Both…. probably (laughter)
The pretending was just a phase really.
I realized pretty quickly that although I fantasized about being a girl,
I was actually a boy;
and heterosexual.
I fancied women, and that made me even more ashamed.
It felt like my body was betraying me.
I didn't want to be a man;
but I was.
I was confused about my sexuality and that made relationships difficult.

Because of my feminine appearance I was bullied
and called a "poofter" at school.
When I was at home I used to think myself into being a "her".
Yet then; I also was scared for my life…

Women were beaten up in my family

With my Nan,
she used to listen to me,
tell me that there was nothing I could do to stop the madness,
that it was up to my Mum.
While I was with her I felt safe.
She believed in me, that I was worth something;
and that I could look after my brother.

I asked her once why she stayed with my grandfather;
she was married for 30 years before he died.

"I was too afraid to leave" she said.
"Also I hated him.
But leaving never really seemed like an option".

I didn't understand.
To me it was logical;
if you hated someone you left.

I did leave the family home as soon as I could.
I couldn't leave without Matthew though..
I waited until he had finished his A levels and gone off into the Army.
Then I left and moved as far away as possible.

Tried to cut thoughts of home and everything out of my mind.

Largely this worked.
I worked my way through college,
got a good job
and met Elizabeth.
We had the children, and only had very fleeting visits home.

All this time though I was dogged by depression.
This kind of heavy blackness that consumed me;
drowned me in nothingness.

Then it happened
the incident with Elizabeth…..
It just took me back to the beginning.
I was just the same as all the other men.

I knew I would never escape.

Sue: But you are here now and talking to me..

I'm wondering what happened?
Did you change your mind?

D: Everyone made such a fuss when I was taken to hospital
I felt really guilty

One of the nurses there gave me a good talking to
told me not to be so selfish…

But one of the cleaners brought me some magazines one day and there was a story in one of them about domestic violence and how he escaped it by having some counselling..

So I guess I thought I'd give it a try.

Email from Sue to Duncan June 2004

Dear Duncan,

It was very good to see you again last week – As requested I have put together some of my thoughts about last week's session. As always, it is only my take on what we talked about, do feel free to correct my interpretation, or disregard anything that is unhelpful.

I was amazed at how well you were able to care for your brother through the many years you lived at home. You spoke of finding cheap food at your local supermarket; they would sometimes give you out of date bread and cakes free, and you spoke of how you always made sure he had some breakfast before going to school; that he was washed and dressed and on the school bus. That must have taken some doing as you were only quite small yourself. You talked a lot about how difficult it was for your mum to cope and how there was never enough money to go round. It sounds as if your mum was very depressed most of the time, and found it really hard to do anything, but you never gave up on her; you always hoped that things would get better. You always remembered, and held onto, the times when she was well, and happy, and sung you and your brothers' folk songs from her native country of Poland.

Some of the things you said made me very sad. The not having enough to eat; never being able to just think about playing like the other boys did; not being able to rely on your mum and dad for things like money; and having to witness such awful violence. I asked you what made you strong enough to bear these things and you said, "I always thought that I could choose to be different when I grew up". I guess this is why you felt so badly when the incident happened with Elizabeth?

It sounds to me though as if you are taking a very different route from your Mum and step-dads though. You are, as you said, "admitting that violence in families is wrong and doing something about it". As I said to you when we were together this takes a great deal of courage but can change things.

Conversations October – December 2004

D: Things changed a lot when we got taken into "care".
We ended up in care for about 18 months.
They couldn't always keep us together;
I went to a family who were lovely,
but they already had three children of their own, and two foster kids.
Matthew went somewhere else.

That wasn't so good.
They complained he wet the bed
and I think some of the other kids their bullied him.
I tried to get Mum to complain,
but she never did.

We were both moved about six times.
That was really hard,
in the end you didn't want to get attached to anyone because
you knew they would dump you again.

Eventually..
We both ended up in a children's home just outside (name deleted).
That was actually not too bad.
Most of the staff were ok,
although, we did get bullied at school.
Matthew wouldn't speak to anyone.
They tried everything;
but he wouldn't even speak to me.

Eventually we went back to live with my mum and nan.
I was 14 then, and Matthew was 9.
It was agreed, on the understanding that my mum lived with nan,
and that she didn't see my step-dad.

Most of the time, she kept to that agreement.
She had major mental health problems by then though.
She would wake us all up in the night sometimes screaming and ranting.
Trying to get us to pack our things and leave because:
"the men" were going to kill her.

She tried to attack me with a knife once..
She didn't recognize who I was.
Nan had to physically restrain her.
I was quite good at the academic stuff and somehow managed to pass my GCSE's and then my A levels.

I was still afraid for Matthew though, so I waited until he was 17 and went into the army and then I left home.

Sue: I'm wondering..
What happened to your relationship with Matthew and your mum and Nan; after you left home?

I tried to forget all about my past and forge a new life.
I went back to see my nan and mum quite often;
well about 3 times a year actually (laughter);
until nan died;
then I stopped visiting much at all.

Mum had got another man in her life
and as far as I could see he was much the same as the previous few.
I did ring her regularly, but I just couldn't go on…
I just couldn't go on witnessing..
the violence;
what it had made her.

Mostly I blotted out the past quite successfully.

When Matthew came home on leave, he usually came to stay with me.
We never ever talked of home..
Never have.

After he had come back from Iraq though, he was discharged with PTSD,
We never talked about that either!
(laughter) Well we are men!

Sue: I wonder whether it would be helpful to talk to him now about all of this?

My suggestion was that perhaps it would be helpful if Matthew was agreeable for them either to meet and talk, or to perhaps write down something of their experiences so that they had a starting point for conversation.

Duncan and Matthew: "Letters about our Past"

Dear Duncan,

Following our phone call I thought it would be good to write some of my feelings down. It is hard for me to talk to you face to face about it because then I just want to cry and feel really ashamed. You have always had such high expectations of me.

I hadn't realized how hard it was for you when we were little. I guess to me, you were always my big brother, who took care of me and I didn't give much thought to how you were coping. I suppose the thing that really still haunts me from that time is the smell of poverty. The smell of unwashed clothes and food scraped together in an unclean kitchen; the smell of blood and urine; the sound of fighting and screaming from above us; the never feeling safe, or worth anything to anyone, apart from you. And ,the anger; it burned inside me all the time.

I spent years hating mother and her men. It really annoyed me that you could forgive her so easily when she was responsible for making our life hell for years. Why could she never resist hooking up with violent men? I guess I am still angry, but having seen a bit more of life I guess I have to just accept that she was damaged and could not help how she was.

Going into the army seemed a really good idea. I was quick to learn, enjoyed the exercises and camaraderie of the squad. I was fearless. Violence was ok here. I was a trained soldier, allowed, encouraged to be aggressive. Also I had already seen enough shit that nothing was likely to shock me.

It was a good life – I travelled the world never really fired a round in a conflict situation until Iraq happened. Even then I felt a confident part of the team. We watched each other's backs. I was reminded of being with you and how when I was a little kid; you looked out for me. The first tour was ok; although several of my colleagues were killed. Then on the second tour several more; others had legs or bits of them blown off and were shot at by nothing more than kids. Then something happened that put me back to being a scared kid. Nothing major, or horrific, just an ordinary day on foot patrol.

Four of us were out at the checkpoint when a group of local men and women started throwing insults (and shit) at us (which was normal in this area). They enjoyed goading us; we were on orders to get alongside the locals and move the Taliban back out of the village. On this day though, one of the men I was out with reacted badly when a local woman spat in his face. He hurled her away from him and struck her across the face. Her child (he must have been 6 or 7) just stood watching, looking at me, not knowing what to do; but the hate in his eyes was there.

I didn't realize at the time but this sent me into a downward spiral. I started shaking all the time, having flashbacks from being a child and watching mother being beaten up. I was unable to concentrate, couldn't sleep, coming out with crazy stuff all the time. Fought with anyone, everyone. My anger was totally out of control. I was unable to do my job basically. When I couldn't hide it any more I was sent back home. That felt like failure and I just wanted to die, but coward that I was, I couldn't even have the balls to do that. That was two years ago and thankfully following lots of therapy, and rehabilitation, I can now see that it was not so much the conflict that caused the problem, but my childhood; the conflict just re-awakened it. I hid from it until that day, when my friend; who I trusted with my life, turned into one of mother's men. Then I was just as fucked up as I was as a child and there was nowhere to run.

I can hear you saying, "why didn't you talk to me" but I guess I didn't want to fail in your eyes; you were the one who believed in me and had managed to get through university and got a wife and child on the way. You were sorted so why wasn't I? And also you never asked me outright. I guess you had your own reasons for wanting to escape the past?

It is a relief to say this all to you now. I am not sure if it makes an awful lot of sense but I hope it doesn't make you feel too bad. I couldn't believe it when I heard you had had some kind of break down. I am sorry I didn't know.

I think back to when we were kids sometimes and wonder what it would have been like if our mother had not had successions of violent relationships?

Hello little Broth,

I have re-read your letter many times and each time it brings a lump to my throat. I guess I am sorry that so much time has passed before we have been able to say these things to each other.

It was good to meet up with you last week – and indeed to sit up talking through the night. It felt like we were finally meeting after being friendly strangers for so long. I am not sure there was anything we could do to change how things were. I think Mum was just stuck in a rut, we couldn't rescue her from it, however hard we tried. I know that you are still really angry with her for allowing this to happen; I have just tried to shut that part of her life out of my consciousness. I think that perhaps you are also angry with me for not being up to the task of taking care of you.

I'm hoping that meeting up regularly to talk now will mean that. We talk. Sue (my counsellor) has said that if we get stuck she is happy to meet with us both, but I think actually, now that we have taken the courage in our hands; we are on a roll so to speak and that we can both help each other to get back on track.

Research Conversations

Over the intervening years both Duncan and Matthew have emailed me from time to time, and when the idea for this book came to light they were enthusiastic to be involved. In 2011 they travelled to meet me in the counselling centre I now work and this is an excerpt of our conversation:

Sue: So, it is a long time since our initial conversations… I am wondering how things have been going for you both and if there is something specific you would like us to talk about today?

Duncan: Yes, it is about 6 years since we last met
and such a lot has happened really.
For me that has mostly been good..
Although I only had a few sessions of counselling;
they were very, very significant in helping me to move on..
and to re-engage with Matthew here!

Matthew: I guess I am amazed to finally be meeting with you.
It has felt as if you have been part of my life for several years now;
we have talked on email and you have been
somehow there, with Dunc and me, when we talk.

Duncan: I guess that my life feels back on track now.
The biggest thing I guess is not feeling so "depressed".
I do get my down moments,
but on the whole the blackness has gone
and I look at life through a different lens.

I did try for a while to talk to Mum about what happened to her,
but she can't, or is not ready, really to talk.
She has been in and out of psychiatric care now for some time
I guess I have just let it go.
I cannot change how things are for her;
only she can do that.
Before, I guess,

I always felt guilty that I couldn't make things better for her.
I still feel really sad about that,
but I can now visit her, and keep her company,
without feeling I am going to disintegrate.
Elizabeth and I are divorced; mostly amicably.
When we were together,
there was just too much anger for me to handle.

I see the children every other weekend; and they are great.
They seem really healthy, and happy,
we do lots of fun things together, which is great.
Elizabeth has a new partner;
he seems a very gentle person, so I am not afraid of violence erupting;
except in myself of course!

Matt and I still meet every week or so,
that's been really important to me over the years.
He gives me a kick up the bum on occasions,
and we now talk about our current life, rather than the past.

Matthew: I agree…
It is good we meet up and talk about life,
politics and relationship possibilities.
We can still talk about the past;
but somehow it is not so relevant as it was.

I still occasionally get troubled with flashbacks;
of both Iraq and childhood,
but they don't consume my life anymore.
I have gone back to college and completed a degree in ecology
and now work for (name deleted).
This means I work outside a lot on projects close to the land
and am for a lot of time my own boss.

I think I still have a problem with anger.
When I get really angry, I get totally out of control….
Then other people sometimes get hurt.

I have done some anger management work with a therapist,
but I am still afraid…
that it will happen again.
So I don't get too close to people usually.
Mother ..
I guess I am not as tolerant of her histrionics as Duncan!
I still see her a couple of times a year;
I definitely do not want to speak

with her about anything meaningful though!

Sue: I guess from our previous conversations, and this one,
that you feel that the trauma of witnessing domestic violence has had a huge impact on your life.
Would it interest you to tell me about that?

Matthew:
Yes. Yes.
Although we weren't physically abused….
The trauma of witnessing what we did,
the terror of knowing
the person that is supposed to protect you,
and fight for you, cannot do it..

It affects everything.
Choices I made in the past;
my going into and being discharged from the army.
It even silenced what we (gestures to Duncan) could talk about.
Silence.
We were silenced
because to talk about it as kids would mean
being removed from our mother
and she was the only parent we had got.

As adults we couldn't talk about it, because it was secret.
No-one could admit it for fear of falling in the pit …

Sue: The pit?

Matthew: Of despair, of chaos.. I mean….

Duncan: I would go even further
We were silenced because this wasn't our secret, it was our mum's.
The only way out
was when we finally were able to talk to each other,
and you…
without it having any impact on our safety, or the safety of our mum.
I had decided as a child that the only safe course as a man,
and as you know I really didn't want to be one! (laughter)
was not to be angry at all…
Of course I know now this was ridiculous.
As you and others have told me,
"anger is a normal emotion",
but it still terrifies me.
I think that is why my marriage failed.

I was too scared of anger;
especially my own.

I have had a few relationships since
but I have tended to walk away when they start to get serious,
or I start feeling too much…

I guess that is the next challenge for me.
Allowing myself to feel everything,
when I am with someone, and feeling safe about it.

Matthew: We do try to help each other out here!
I guess I also find it hard to trust people
enough to let them into my life.

When the one person,
who is supposed to be there for you,
lets you down..
Yes… before you say anything Duncan..
I know she was a victim too!
There is something within you that rejects anyone getting too close.
Except for him of course … (laughter)

I suppose growing up with violence, unlike Duncan,
I just adopted it as a way to behave.
I'm not proud of it…
But it is a difficult habit to get out of.

Sue: Do you think this will change?

Matthew: I think it has changed, and continues to change,
as we talk about it.
Even talking with you, here today,
makes it seem more possible.
I can talk about feeling angry; without actually experiencing anger.
That's a new first for me!

Duncan: And we talked all the way down here in the car too.
I guess one day you might talk to us and we'll be totally sorted!!

We talked generally for a while about the research project and the book I was involved with writing; and how they might like to be involved. They decided that as well as including some of their past conversations, they would like to write something together. Following many drafts written individually then together this is what they have come up with:

Violence breeds in secret corners
fuelled by silent screams.
Traumatized women give birth to
traumatized children
who grow into traumatized adults.
Violence lurks in the dark recesses
waiting like a thief in the night
for the right moment
to assert his dominance.

> A woman screams,
> blood runs down her face,
> she is out of her mind with terror
> while the frozen children look on.

Violence leaves a legacy;
an inheritance of hate and fear
which impregnate and infiltrate
the mind and being of the generation to come.
When will it stop?
With me?
With my children's children?
Or will it go on generation after generation?

CHAPTER FIVE

JASON

One of the contracts I held for three years was to provide anger management/counselling sessions to people, referred by social services; these were all young men who had often been involved in situations of domestic violence and child protection issues. Court proceedings were always part of the agenda. Often the court would make an order which required the council to ensure that the perpetrator of the violence received anger management before any contact was granted for the man or woman to live with, or unrestricted visiting with, his children. I had to provide social services with a report detailing our work together.

When I first took this contract on many of my colleagues were surprised. I often worked with victims of domestic violence; they found it hard to understand how I, a middle aged woman, was going to be able to adapt my working style to meet meaningfully with these young men, and also how I was going to adapt my then very person centred approach to such a prescriptive discipline. I was not sure either! I knew however that the key to stopping violence in families was finding out what was going on in these volatile situations, and finding ways to give both those who were victims, and perpetrators of violence, some tools to find different ways of living I also recognised that perpetrators were not always men; women also crossed the line between, feeling angry, and physically assaulting another.

I agreed to see the men in the local community centre, and under the guidance of my supervisor ensured that I had strategies for keeping myself safe; which included an alarm and a caretaker who policed the waiting room, "I won't take any funny business" he commented the first time I arrived. I think after a few weeks he relaxed a little, and so did I. I never had any problems with the people I was working with being violent, or even angry. Terrified men, subdued in their manner, waited docilely for me in the waiting room. One man was so afraid; he felt the only way he could be in the same room as me, and talk, was if he was allowed to smoke. This meant our sessions took place in the, "smoker's room" which for me, a non-smoker, was close to torture. We did not seem to be connecting on any real level. Yes they were attending, I was adopting the role of teacher, and with the aid of cognitive behaviour techniques was enabling them to find strategies for coping when their, "anger boiled over" as one man put it. They were all reluctant to talk about the anger, mostly minimising its effect on them and their families. Reports were collaborative and demonstrated their willingness to engage, but what was missing was any indication of the anger, or as Jason said to me "the rage that burns me out" or how to change things on more than just a surface level.

There are many theories regarding anger and violence. Many have considered domestic violence to be all about patriarchal power and control (Buzawa and Buzawa 2002) and gender injustice that permeates society. Other studies have shown that the violence is not limited to males, but there is also a high level of violence between females, and against men by women (Dutton and Nichols 2006). All of us experience anger; some, often women, find it a hard emotion to express as culturally within western societies it is not seemly for a woman to be angry; often however it helps motivate people to make changes. Within my work I am not so much interested in theoretical, models, but of enabling people to re-author (White 1995) their lives in different ways. Ways that perhaps do not include violence. Around this time however I was also undertaking study at the University of Bristol; one of my fellow students, Sue Parker Hall was making a study of anger and rage; her theoretical standpoint interested me. She was putting forward the idea that rage was very different from anger. She explains what she means at the beginning of her subsequent book: "anger is a pure emotion, a vital piece of intelligence about the immediate environment that we are in"(Parker-Hall 2009). She considers anger therefore vital in the process of relating to others and providing the energy to negotiate the "human and relational path between dependence and independence" (ibid:1). Rage however, she claims is a totally different psychological process; emanating from a much earlier developmental stage and is, "not an emotion at all but a trauma related defence mechanism evoked when a person is overwhelmed by their experience and cannot integrate it"(ibid:2). It is this kind of rage that she sees as being responsible for much of the domestic, and societal, violence we see in society.

As she was talking about all of this, I made some connections between what she was saying, and what I knew about PTSD and peoples responses to trauma. Were these young men I was working with affected by childhood trauma? If so, could this rage be a kind of defence; a similar response to dissociating or other responses to trauma I had witnessed?

If rage is a response to trauma, and an inability to process the memory of a life experience, or experiences, then the therapeutic key may be in enabling that person to re-connect, and re-story, that experience in some kind of way. This could only, I felt, be done through relationship, and this had to be more than just a meeting to discuss cognitive strategies; more was needed than was happening in the current sessions which I was running.

At this time I was also starting to learn about narrative therapy techniques, and I wondered whether these would help at all.

I remember a distinct turning point in my work with one man. He sat guardedly with his arms folded and answered my questions about his life with yes's and no's, nearly always in the right place, but when I moved away from the incident and asked about his life experiences and encouraged him to externalise (Dale 2009) "rage" asking questions such as, "how long has 'rage' been part of your life?" and asking him to tell me some of the stories of his life. He went on to tell me about his childhood; stories I cannot include here as I have subsequently lost contact with him. I was in no doubt that for this man, at least, early trauma had resulted in him using "rage" as an escape.

Because I felt it would be helpful to include a story from someone who has experienced this kind of overwhelming rage; and I had no client material that I could use, I advertised for contributors in BACP's counselling journal Therapy Today. My reasoning was that only counsellors/psychotherapists, or students of these disciplines, read this journal so if someone contacted me they would be more likely to have training and support strategies if conversations with me awakened feelings that were difficult to process, or cope with, in the process of a research project.

Jason emailed me. He was a counsellor on the final year of a diploma training course. He had trained to become a counsellor in light of his experience of receiving counselling. He had come through a very difficult relationship break up, where he had been physically violent towards his partner. Like all the contributors has had the choice of keeping his name, or choosing a pseudonym. After careful thought, has decided to write under a pseudonym. He says, "I am who I am now, the story I live by now is not what happened in the past. I have lived through that, unfortunately so have others, but they like me know that I live my life differently, but they have not the choices I have about writing this stuff". Together we explore aspects of his story and how he has managed to make changes, and look at issues regarding gender justice; what it means to him now to be a man living by different stories.

I asked Jason if he wanted to tell me his story, or whether he would like to write it. What follows is his writing and our subsequent conversations arising from this writing:

Jason – May 2012

I suppose my first memories are of violence. I do not say that as an excuse, merely as a fact. I remember my father, who was normally a mild mannered man, drunk raging at my mother. Usually it built up over a period of weeks; something that my mother did, or said, would mean he became irritable, picked faults in cooking, washing, anything he could think about. If we, my sister and I, were foolish enough to not keep out of the way we were liable to be on the receiving end of a clip round the ear (this was usually carried out with a shoe or slipper, or anything to hand). During these times we lived on eggshells. We knew it was all going to blow, but we didn't know when. The next phase was the drinking. He would go to the pub after work and steadily get drunk. When he returned late in the evening he would start on at mother calling her a whore, a cunt, anything hurtful he could find to say. She would quietly try to avoid the conflict. It always escalated and usually ended with her being either beaten or raped. I will give you an example. One Friday night (name deleted) and I returned from school to find my mother tied up in the outside lavatory. She was bleeding and had no clothes. We managed between us to get her back to the house. She would never say anything about my father though. She always spoke of him as if he was a God and she had deserved what had happened. After one of these "blow ups" there was always a period of calm; he was always remorseful; bringing her flowers and chocolates; speaking to her as if she was a princess.

My sister and I just kind of ignored it; one day however my mother left; when we came home from school we found her gone. Just a note left on the dresser. What would my father do? We waited silently for him to return, and when he did, scuttled to our rooms and listened for him to find the note? The trauma of that forever haunts me; he blamed us; (name deleted) especially. I started to blame her too; along with my mother. I look at it now and feel deeply ashamed that I did not protect her; that I turned into a model of my father. It felt safe to jeer at her and side with my father. Learning about transactional analysis now I realise I felt that "I was ok" and she was very definitely "not ok"(Harris 1995).

I didn't go to university or college, but into an apprenticeship with a local firm of motor mechanics. I found this a very masculine place where it was fine to joke about women, and girly pictures appeared on the walls of the canteen. Women were thought to be fair game for banter, sexual advances and all of us would try to encourage the girls in the office to wear short skirts and revealing clothing.

I met my wife Lillian (pseudonym) when I was 22. I went to the local club which held a disco once a week, and there she was, beautiful her long hair and brown eyes trusting me to look after her. I went into marriage hoping for the world. I vowed to love, cherish and look after her until death us do part. We lived in a small terrace house that we rented from my boss. We were happy for a glorious eighteen months until our daughter was born, and then two years later my son. Even now after much therapy and talking I am nor really sure what happened. I could feel myself getting tetchy. I hated myself for it, and her more for seeing it and accepting it. Then one night I went to the pub after work and got drunk; I came back to find that she was not there. There was a note on the table, "Dear Jason, I have taken the children to see the Christmas lights being switched on. Help yourself to eggs and bacon for supper". Something inside me just flicked into a place where I did not exist any more. There was only this kind of rage. I wanted to destroy anything and everything. I started with the kitchen; destroying the door of the fridge; emptying the contents over the kitchen. I found a bottle of whisky to drink, and by the time she got back with the children I was completely unconscious.

This was the start of it. Soon these violent episodes escalated. I became violent towards Lilli; I was completely out of control. Afterwards the shame and the repulsion made me drink more, and this fuelled yet more violence.

Eventually, after I had broken her arm and two ribs, in front of the children, she reported me to the police. In some ways this felt like betrayal, but I think that it actually saved my life; and probably hers. I was one of the few who are prosecuted for domestic violence; most women apparently drop the charges. Lillian was determined however; I was so proud of her. I received a custodial six month sentence. The shock of that was huge; but in some ways it was the best thing that has ever happened to me; it enabled me to stop, and make changes. If I had carried on as I was I would have killed someone. I have to live everyday with the memory of what I did, but this is nothing compared to what Lillian has to live with, and my children, the terror of that.

I want here to try to talk about what was going on in these outpourings of rage and violence. I feel if I can understand what is happening with my mind and body I will have a better chance of changing what happens and others may also gain insight.

Usually in the days leading up to an incident there are some changes in my thinking. Obsessive thoughts start to run through my mind. These are completely contrary to my normal thoughts and belief system. For example whilst married I would catch a glimpse of Lillian laughing with a friend, and a random thought such as, "when I'm dead she'll be having sex with other men" would go through my mind. Immediately I would try to squash it. I knew it was irrational, not based on any facts, but the thought though would never go away. It would come back to me throughout the day and night; embroidered, and although I knew on one level that it was not true, it would become an obsession. However I tried to escape it, I would find myself over the next few days, thinking on it. I also then found it difficult to connect with anyone around me. Lillian would start to irritate me. I could feel myself becoming snappy, finding fault.

This would inevitably lead to escalation. She would become more distant with me, trying to avoiding the conflict. Drinking would often fuel the building feeling of tension within me. Then the incident would start; it could be a word, an intrusive thought. I would feel a tingling at the back of my neck, my mouth feeling dry, and it would be difficult to swallow. My ears would ring and seem to burn. At this point I would be conscious of my heart pumping faster than normal. Sometimes I was aware of a metallic taste in my mouth.

If it got to this point then a kind of burning would take over the whole of my being; not just my body; and fury erupts. All I want to do at that point is destroy anything in my path; especially the person standing in front of me.

I have thought about this long and hard, and I am not sure that I consciously think anything. I have questioned, is it about power and control? Is it inherited from my father? Am I just a really evil person who cannot be in relationship with others? Do I do this consciously to maintain my position in a relationship? I am not sure that actually it is any of these, but they could have some bearing on it. It is more like a very primitive response. My feelings sometimes seem more akin to being afraid than angry. I am angry when someone at work fucks up, but that is a very conscious process. I am in control of the anger; it is about loss; sometimes of status, other times of revenue. I feel let down. It has nothing to do with this other experience which is like drowning. Some may see this as a, "cop out" of my responsibility and avoidance of guilt; but I don't think that it is that either. I am fully aware and ashamed of my behaviour; I just need to understand it so that I can change.

With help from my therapist I now anticipate what is happening quickly. I have got better at reading the signs and have found breathing techniques and self-hypnosis techniques which stop it escalating. I am too afraid to have a proper relationship though. I know that it is still there, lurking, like a cancer; one day it will overwhelm me again. I will become Frankenstein. I am afraid of what I might do.

Conversations with Jason

Meeting with Jason over coffee in Wales near where I live; we talk about what he has written, the forthcoming book, and how the stories change.

Sue: I guess that I am really interested in your thoughts about this being a "primitive reaction" and more like "fear". Would you like to say a bit more about that?

Jason: Yes. It feels like fear.
Which is crazy because it comes out as violence.
It's like something switches gear in my brain…
Over a period of a few days everything I thought I knew about changes.
Like putting on a pair of glasses with different lenses;
the whole world looks and is experienced by me as different.
People I thought I knew suddenly seem to be quite bizarre.
Trust goes.
I cannot find any part of me that trusts,
or feels safe.
Everything is so terrifying.
All the familiar landmarks are taken away.
It sounds really stupid……
It feels like living in a completely separate universe.
I can see the people I care about living just as they always do..

I just cannot reach out and touch them.

Sue: How long does this kind of experience go back?
I mean is it something that recently happened to you as an adult,
or did it happen at all when you were small?

Jason: I think I lived in that place a lot when I was small.

Especially after my mother went.
Nothing felt safe.
The way I was….
I was a quiet shy child;
this child could not cope with life that was left after she went.
I still cannot bear to think of it…..

It didn't come out as violence then.
But there are periods of my life where I was absent.
I know from photos and things that I was there.
I have no memories of them;
neither of the photo's being taken, or the life that surrounded them,
I was just absent.
Somewhere else in a different world.

Sometimes when I was a teenager I used to cut my arms;
just to feel something I think..
I can't really remember why…..

Sue: It sounds a difficult place to be…..

Jason: Yes…..(weeps silently)
I have talked about this before in therapy,
but it feels somehow that as a man I shouldn't feel it so much;
and as the perpetrator of domestic violence
I should never receive compassion.

Sue: Do you think any of this is about gender issues;
I mean how you see your masculinity,
and how you see women's femininity?

Jason: I think that my father and mother's attitudes about what women,
and men, should be; has a lot to do with it.
He was a "real man";
or so he thought.
My mother,
he thought,
ought to do what he willed.

I am pretty sure that it was because I never could live up to what he
expected of a, "real son" that I went to this other place.
And now it is a place I spring back to on automatic rewind.

I thought when I got married that I had sussed what it meant to be a;
"gentle" man.
I was never going to be like my father.

How naïve I was.

Sue: Sometimes it sounds as if you feel stuck with a label that you do not want or like?

Jason: Yes. Stuck with, “perpetrator of violence”, “criminal”.
I try so hard to live life in different ways.

Sue: I would really like to hear about those different ways? What life would look like without those labels I wonder?

Jason: I see myself as having relationships where I do not retreat into this “other” place. Relationships based on who I want to be.
Being a man who respects others;
seeing women as equal with all the needs, desires, quirks that men have.
Being a man who is loved;
for who I am, where I am at the present.
Being a man who is afraid;
yet does not retreat out of view.
Being a man who looks with a woman’s eyes at those around me.

Sue: How would you know that you have become that man?

Jason: When I can have conversations like this without retreating.
When I can have challenging conversations with other women without retreating.

Years ago, we could have never have been able to have these kind of conversations.
I would have been gone…...
I would have started to go into that place
and the rage would have come.

Sue: What enables you to stay now…
I mean what has changed so that you can stay now.

Jason: A real determination to change,
continuing to talk about these issues;
even though it is tough.
Knowing that you are not judging me.

Not wanting to ever be again the monster I was.
I looked in the mirror, so to speak, when I was in prison.
I saw what I would become if I carried on that way.

It is not easy though.
He lurks ready to pounce at any moment.

Sue: I am very glad that you have stayed to speak with me.

Jason: It feels life changing that you are prepared to listen,
and that I can become part of something bigger than just me.
That my experience, and that of Lillian's,
which was so terrible for her,
Can change things in some way.

I wish I could change things that happened.
I am deeply ashamed of my behaviour….

This is only a short excerpt from our conversation, but it hopefully gives insight into a different perspective on domestic violence. We decided as this was going to be published to write to Lillian (pseudonym) in order to gain permission for Jason to share this story. We were both aware that Lillian had been very hurt by Jason's behaviours, and may not feel comfortable either with our conversations, or their inclusion within this book. We agreed that if she felt she would rather his narrative not be included, we would abide by her wishes.

Here is her reply:

Dear Susan,

Thank you so much for your letters, and the enclosed chapters in your forthcoming book. I really resonated with all that was said – especially the writings by Duncan and Matthew. I was also touched, even though I did not want to be, by what Jason had to say.

I am so glad that he is addressing the issues he has had in the past with violence. It took everything for me to report him to the police. I loved him. I could not however continue to live with him and in constant fear. Especially when it was witnessed by the children; even though they were small they are still really sensitive to angry voices. He used to turn into this person I just did not know. This eventually killed everything, and would have killed me if I had stayed.

I always knew that there was something really traumatic about Jason's past, not that I see this as an excuse; and I do not feel this is being offered by you, or him, as an excuse. This seems like a genuine act by him of trying to become the Jason he has it within himself to be. My Jason. The Jason I knew and married.

I have now remarried and the children think of their step-father as dad, although they know about Jason, and I guess one day, when they are older, they may want to meet with him.

I would be grateful if you could keep my name anonymous, and I do not want to have further contact with him. You are however welcome to print this letter. It is perhaps important for women who are subjected to domestic violence to know that **it is right to take action**; even if you love him. Sometimes it is the only way to change things. Life will not end because you have left, and sometimes it makes you a stronger person.

I have always felt, deep down, guilty that I could not help Jason, now I realise that by reporting him I probably have. I wish him, and you, well.

Part II

Spiritual and Religious Settings

CHAPTER SIX

SEXUAL ABUSE WITHIN THE CHURCH

As human beings we are drawn to questions of spirituality. Whether these questions about spirituality are supported by a specific faith or religious understanding, or are more of an existential searching for meaning outside the physical confines of being human, most of us at some point in our lives ask such things as, "is there more to life than this"; "what is the meaning of suffering"; "why is the world such a beautiful yet savage place". These questions and answers shape our central beliefs about ourselves, our relationships, our morality, how we view others and how we interact with the world.

The major religions of Christianity, Judaism, Islam, Buddhism, Hinduism, Sikhism have over two millennia supported people to understand more about their faith and spiritual journey. People trust those appointed by these organisations to be committed to the wellbeing of members. When something goes wrong however and those appointed in positions of trust abuse those in their care; whether this be by physical, sexual or even spiritual abuse then the results can be devastating. The injuries done are not just to the body and the mind, but also within the relationship the person has with their sense of spirituality, with God and with other people.

Within this chapter my intention is to look briefly at abuse within Christian communities. This is not because I believe there is never abuse within other religious communities, or that the "church" is somehow more prone to abuse than other religions, but is because it is from within this specific setting that two co-researchers have brought their stories and within the UK Christianity is the main religion. A survey in 2007 showed 53% of the adult population in the UK claiming to be Christian compared with 6% belonging to other faiths and 39% who claim to have no formal religion (Ashworth and Farthing 2007).

Firstly I intend to look briefly at what the main church denominations have to say about how they provide guidance and protection policies to safeguard vulnerable and young people in their care. Secondly to explore some of the possible effects to the person, and subsequent generations of sexual abuse when it takes place within a church setting.

The church is more than just one organisation. Within the UK there are many different denominations each with its own policies and governance. Within a survey conducted by Tear Fund in 2007 of church attendance it was shown that 27% of adults described themselves as Anglican, 30% as Roman Catholic 16% as Presbyterian, 4% Baptist, 5% Methodist, 5% Pentecostal, 3% Independent, 3% Charismatic, 5% Orthodox and 2% Other (Ashworth and Farthing 2007). For the purposes of this book I am going to look specifically at the policies relating to the two largest churches mentioned above; the Anglican Church, specifically the Church of England, and the Roman Catholic Church.

In the 1980's reports of widespread sexual abuse by Catholic priests across the world started to make their way into the media. People, both Christians and non Christians alike shocked both by the nature and prevalence of the abuse, and that often abuse had been covered up by church leaders. It emerged that the Catholic hierarchy did not always report allegations of abuse to civil authorities, and often just moved the accused priest to a new location, often where they still had contact with young people, and in this way avoided the danger of scandal. Currently the Catholic Church has committed to investigate and hold to account those who have been involved in historic abuse cases, and to ensure policies and checks are in place such that young people are protected from potential abuse. The time taken to take acknowledge that there were indeed issues to be addressed, and delayed action in dealing with these issues by the church hierarchy have however tainted public opinion and lessened the trust in the ability of the church to act effectively in these matters. The Cumberlege Commission Report (Wales 2007) states:

> "It has taken time for the Church to realise fully the implications of this betrayal by clergy and lay people working in the Catholic Church and to learn how to respond fairly, properly and supportively. In 2000 Cardinal Cormac Murphy-O'Connor invited Lord Nolan to set a framework for best practice and prevention to assist the Church to do just that".

Lord Nolan's recommendations also included that there be a further review hence the production of the Cumberlege Commission Report. These conclude with a number of recommendations for the Church to implement in order to safeguard young people and vulnerable adults.

Within the Church of England the first policy document for the protection of children appeared in 1995 and has been subsequently updated in 2004 and 2007 when the Church of England's House of Bishop's issued a policy document (2007) calling for a review of all historic cases of child abuse which has now been carried out throughout each diocese[1]. The review reported:

> "As a result of the diocesan reviews of 40,747 files, 13 cases were identified requiring formal action. Eleven cases were referred to the statutory authorities, eight of which involved a member of the clergy and three of which involved a non-ordained person holding some form of church office. Five of these cases relate to past allegations that originally involved police investigation and some of which resulted in convictions" (ChurchofEngland 2010)

Further extensive policies have now been developed in the Church of England (2010) and each church, that is a member of this denomination, has to have a child protection policy and a child protection officer appointed who undertakes to oversee the protection of the young and vulnerable.

Is this enough though? I guess these policies and ongoing vigilance will help to lessen the chances of people (both clergy and laity) being able to abuse young people within church settings and the historic reviews have redressed some level of justice to those abused in the past, although there are some who have questioned:

> "whether the Church has been submitted to the kind of scrutiny it should rightly receive, and whether incidents of cover-up and/or serious incompetence were restricted to isolated incidents affecting a very small minority, or were parts of a wider church problem" (Merrick 2011)

Unfortunately there will always be those who seek employment within organizations where they can gain access to those who are most vulnerable within society, but at least there are now within the mainstream churches, and most statutory and charitable organizations, safeguarding strategies such that at least people with known histories of criminal activity and abuse can be identified. The time, even within the churches, where a "blind eye" could be cast over accusations of child abuse has I hope

---

[1] A diocese contains all the churches that are under the authority of one bishop, or the district containing them.

passed. However, even as I write this chapter a further critical report has been published about Chichester diocese, which has left the diocese under special measures and where, "disastrous dysfunctionality" enabled clergy with records of sexually abusing children still working within parishes.[2] Many of the smaller denomination of churches also have put in place good policies, as have smaller house churches, or religious communities. Without the organisational structures in place to monitor and evaluate, the small house churches and religious communities often find child and vulnerable adult protection, in a formal way, difficult to implement.

Going back to Salter's words about abusers leaving "footprints in the mind" (Salter 1995:3) of their victims, I want to look further at what kind of impact being abused within a religious setting could have on a person, and their families lives.

Research (McLaughlin 1994; Fater and Mullaney 2000; Disch and Avery 2001) shows clearly the negative effect of sexual abuse by clergy (or those appointed by churches to positions of trust). Survivors in the Fater and Mullaney study describing a "bifurcated rage and spiritual distress that pervades their 'lifebeing'" (Fater and Mullaney 2000:281) How, I wonder does this rage and spiritual distress transmit to the following generations. The following commentary is based on conversations with two contributors who contacted me following an advertisement for research contributors within a counselling journal. They both described themselves as survivors of childhood sexual abuse in church settings. Both were trainee counsellors and had families of their own. I hope that this gives a unique glimpse into the way in which abuse in a church setting could affect the wider family.

As children we have to trust the people who have responsibility for our lives, our parents, our teachers, those who have responsibility for us. How we grow up and relate to others depend on these very early relationships. Within Christian families the teachings of Christ, the church, are central. To be told as a child that, "God is love" and yet to be told by the clergyman (or woman) that, "God will only love us if we keep secrets" (Helen) or that "it is because you are really bad that God is allowing me to

---

[2] For more information on this report, and the church recommendations see http://www.diochi.org.uk/index.cfm?fuseaction=activities.content&cmid=637#recommendations

punish you" (Joanne) has an effect on how we see ourselves, and also how we see God. Joanne goes on to say:

> "I was about twelve years old, and this really respected, well liked person, who was almost parent like, was telling me that I was being punished for being a 'bad' person. My body apparently was not what Jesus would have wanted to see. God would never forgive me if I could not change it. The results were that I grew up outwardly a very quiet good Christian girl, and inside my head hated myself. I used to scrub my body in the bath with a kitchen scourer to stop my breasts from looking as they did. I had this image of God, which is still there I suppose, as like that man. He will never forgive me. I will always be a sinner. I know logically with my adult brain that this cannot possibly be true, but somewhere even driving past a church building, or listening to a clergyman speak on the news I am back there with the scourer."

Although it is true that traditional approaches to church and religion are becoming less popular, as Swinton points out:

> "whilst people may be becoming less *religious* it would be a mistake to assume from that that they are necessarily becoming less *spiritual*, or that they are no longer searching for a sense of transcendence and spiritual fulfilment"(Swinton 2001:11).

People are, and continue to be, spiritual beings. As a counsellor more and more people come asking questions such as: "What is the point in this life?"; "surely there must be more to life than this?" "What is going to happen to me when I die?" These questions, existential in nature draw all of us, religious or not, into relationship with others and a universal divine spirit. As psychiatrist Powell comments,

> "I have a vision of a participative cosmos in which I am in limitless relation to the greater whole, the *anima mundi*, indeed the *anima universale*" (Powell 2012:14)

When our relationships with spirituality have footprints of sexual abuse; caused by representatives of the very organisations which have been set up to represent relationships with God, what effect does this have on the person? Helen comments:

> "Because he represented Christ on earth, I have taken with me everywhere this kind of schizophrenic image of him. He is non-judgmental, loving and yet commits terrible atrocities. Speaking about these atrocities I know that I will die, and I will be condemned to eternal hell fire".

I asked both Helen and Joanna what this meant for their families. Joanna says,

> "My mother and father always talked about how amazing HE was. I was silenced by their adoration, and also by their belief in purity and chastity. I was never allowed out on the town, or to wear lewd makeup, or revealing clothes. There was such a deep contrast between their beliefs and what was happening to me. I could never have told them. They would be shocked beyond belief, and I could not bear their disgust in me".

Helen says,

> "I could never have told my mother or father, it would have killed them. Their belief in God was everything. I also thought that because the priest was so powerful, and God was in him, that they would never believe me."

They go on to talk about their own relationships with partners and children. Joanna says:

> "Sexually I was very promiscuous. For my age, I knew how to use sexuality to get my own way with the boys. When I met Simon (my husband) it felt very different, and I have talked to him a lot. But it has caused difficulties for us sexually. I also think I am so anti-God now that it affects my children ever exploring that area of their life. Even though I try not to over-react; when the school has assembly, or homework etc, I just feel really awful about it and the children of course know. I also feel sad that I cannot allow them to go off on a guide camp or such thing.
>
> I long sometimes to be more trusting of people, to take them on face value, but you cannot un-learn the habits of a lifetime. My way of keeping myself and my children safe is to be ultra vigilant. I do realise however that this may have an effect on my children; hopefully this will however be less harmful than abuse.
>
> I think this has affected my family, indelibly. I think that I could have been someone very different if it had not happened to me. I think I could have been a different mother.
>
> Growing up, as I did, where God was central to everything, I grew up with fear, and that fear has never gone away; of being judged and condemned by Him. My parents were such dear, caring people, they genuinely believed in this loving caring God. I knew Him however through the priest. He was not loving or caring. Even after years and years of personal counselling and soul searching I still have nightmares. I have tried to hate God. He did after all send his own son to his death, and instructed

> Abraham to sacrifice his! His ministers do continue to abuse children in their care. Why should I care about Him? I have to keep my children safe, and He does not represent safety. Yet, in saying that I know I am depriving them of becoming spiritual beings."

Helen goes on to say:

> "My children, my daughter especially, have a very hard time. I know that I go on at her to 'keep her safe' so much so that she rolls her eyes, well she is twelve! I am also terrified when she starts to go about with short skirts, or wear makeup. She does not see the dangers. I know I am overreacting, but I can't seem to help it. I never want her to know what happened to me. I am ashamed I suppose. When I was young I did not act out my feelings. I coped at the time by being extra good, extra quiet, but inside I wanted to scream, and scream, and rage. It feels sometimes as if she is doing the screaming and raging for me. I am not sure how that happened; whether she picked something up from me, from my behaviour. I have after all never talked to her about the details of what happened to me. I did however, after one major flare up, where she lied about where she had been and came back drunk, try to explain a little bit about why I was being so strict, I didn't tell her the details, only that someone my parents trusted had abused me as a child, and I did not want her to go through that. Since then, she has asked me the occasional question, and challenged me when she thinks I am 'getting too paranoid' but on the whole she seems better, and I seem better with her.
>
> My husband does know more, though again I have never talked about it more than in general terms. I never go to church now the whole 'religion' thing makes me feel quite sick. I do not consider myself a Christian, and I suppose it has put me off looking at any kind of spiritual or religious thoughts. This I suppose is sad in one sense, but I also think that it is positive in that I tend to live for today rather than being worried about a better life to come".

As shown in previous chapters the effects of sexual abuse on our thoughts, feelings and behaviours is profound. When this is combined with issues of spirituality it is often overwhelming. It would be difficult, however hard a parent tries, for these extreme feelings never to permeate through to the next generation. Sometimes the trauma is so great that even flashbacks trouble children who are unaware of the abuse causing them. It is now being found, especially in combat veterans children, PTSD symptoms can result in those children "exhibiting varying degrees of emotional, psychological and behavioural manifestations of the parent's traumatic experience" (Leiner 2009).

Helen and Joanna had both responded to an advertisement for participants placed in a counselling journal and I was curious about what they hoped to gain from their participation, and whether they had gained anything from the experience.

Helen says:

"As I train to be a counsellor I learn more and more about myself, and I hope that one day I will be able to talk to my daughter about what happened in ways that do not traumatise her, but enable her (and me) to move forward. Being part of this writing, and learning about other people's experiences I am totally committed to that, and I also feel much less alone with something that had previously felt like the world's best kept secret, somehow together we are creating a tapestry of something different."

Joanna confirms:

"I guess this was not really an altruistic thought of helping with your research, but part of my own quest for understanding my own story, and being able to start to break away from the secret power of abuse.

Counselling training kind of focus's the mind on working on your own stuff before you work with clients, and also the effect a parent has on their child. This is hopefully the start of me trying to find a way through all of this. Reading the other people's contributions is just so helpful and gives me hope that there is a future for me and my family outside the power that something that happened so long ago has exerted on my family. The abuse I feel should stop with me, and not go on into the future generations".

CHAPTER SEVEN

WRITING WITH PATRICK

Letters about my life – Patrick

Dear Sue,

You asked me to write something about what brought me to your counselling room. I am not sure whether what I have written is worth reading! but here goes.

I knew from an early age that I was somehow called towards God and the spiritual. I am not sure how I knew, but something about the stories about belief and faith used to really resonate with me, and made sense of a world I often experienced as chaotic. I was one of the sad few who actually enjoyed religious studies at school. I also realised from a very early age that although my mum used to take me to church (she was a Catholic and attended weekly mass), my father never attended, and God was never to be spoken about in our house; apart from at Christmas when cards symbolising virgin births were hung round the house there were never any outward signs of Christianity.

I guess, as most young people growing up in the late sixties and seventies experienced, "being religious" was not a popular option and I put those kind of thoughts on the back burner. I tried to fit in with what was expected of me from my peers and also from my father. He worked at the university teaching graduates chemistry; his assumption was that I would do my A levels, then go off to university to study, "a serious academic subject". I didn't disappoint, having got A grades I set off for London and a degree in medicine. I really struggled. It is hard to bring back the feelings from then, but I guess predominately it was one of drowning. It got tougher and tougher. I started to drink and take amphetamines to get me through. I also experimented (as most of my compatriots did) with LSD, cannabis and something we called the "green giant" concocted by one of the students on a pharmaceutical course and really went off the rails. During this time I was having major panic attacks.

During this time I also started to have serious thoughts of suicide, but never really acted on those thoughts. Then one day on my way to the hospital I noticed the lights on in a neighbouring church and went in. It was a Church of England fairly middle of the road communion service. Following the service the priest shook my hand and said, “come and see me some time if you want to talk” and gave me directions to the vicarage. I went, and it was the start of a very different phase of my life. All of a sudden I felt accepted and part of something. Much to my parents upset I ceased my studies in medicine and enrolled on a theology degree.

I just loved the studying, the discussions, the worship, the relationships I had with those around me. I graduated with a first and then took some time out to consider what my tutors called “my calling”. I knew without a shadow of a doubt I was being called into the priesthood. Following a period of voluntary work and attending various churches in the area I applied for consideration of ordination in the Church of England. This means undertaking various tasks, and culminating in attending a regional then national selection conference. I was successful and following training, was ordained in the summer of 1989. Both my mother and father came. My father wept.

My first posting was as a curate to a very busy inner London parish. I loved it. I helped to run youth groups, prayer groups, preached about once a month. Took the occasional funeral and generally liaised with various community faith groups. There was a team of four of us, and I felt really valued there and supported in my ministry. During this time I met and married my wife Jane.

When I had served my curacy I decided to go back up to Yorkshire and took on responsibility for three country churches. This was much tougher and I noticed that I was often working 60 hour weeks. Jane was pregnant and finding living in a rural community really hard. So much was expected of her as the “rector’s wife”. As the months turned into years I started to slip down into depression. I couldn’t see God – I couldn’t actually see anything hopeful in the world. Everything went into greyness. Even my children didn’t seem to penetrate the wall of grey between us.

I struggled on; slipping further and further down. Nothing in life seemed worth living for. I preached the gospel, said my prayers, listened to the dying and the aggrieved and occasionally read a bedtime story to my children. I reached into a different kind of spirituality, the kind that comes in a bottle with a bird on the label!

No-one from the community or the church seemed to notice. I noticed their not noticing however; within me despair turned to contempt, and contempt turned to hate. Mainly hate for myself, but also for the church.

In 2006 it all came to a head. My wife left with the children and I was alone. I am not sure what happened, I think I got drunk and tried to drive to one of the churches to take a service; I don't really remember. I was involved in an accident involving another car and the police were called. I was prosecuted for drink driving, lost my licence and resigned from my parish.

I moved to Wales to get away from my demons, but unfortunately they travelled (unwanted) with me. I tried to plan my demise, but for some unknown reason I couldn't do it. I kept having these really violent religious dreams where I am kneeling in a church vestry and the priest is smothering me with purple. I eventually ended up at the local medical centre. My GP gave me anti-depressants and suggested counselling. I wasn't very keen, but I really did not have many other options.

So that is what brings me to your door!

Patrick's Journal

31.3.09

My counsellor Sue seems sure after reading my first literary efforts that I ought to keep a journal – or rather she didn't say ought but, "wondered whether it would be helpful" such politically correct clap trap that seems to stop her making any useful suggestions. She gave me a little notebook and a purple pen – purple! I ask you. The colour for a papist!!

She asked me if, "it would interest me" to write about what I felt in response to our sessions. Pah…. Nothing. Well not; nothing. Angry.

Angry but not sure why?

Just angry. Can't write. Going to gym to work out my frustrations on the machine before I crack open a bottle for consolation.
More nightmares and panic attacks. Not sure what causes them

8.4.09

Dear Diary,
Another week passes. Still feel the same. Angry.
I suppose that is a change from "depressed" which was why I was sent to counselling in the first place. Depression stops me feeling. It is a state of non-being. Just dead inside. Sometimes I wonder why I didn't die, but I realise that I just couldn't be bothered. At least now I've got the energy even if I am not sure the will.

Not sure why I am rambling on. A sense of duty? boredom? Complete waste of time.

22.4.09

New regime planned for the day:
6.30 Get up eat breakfast
7.0 Go to gym
8.30 Arrive at work (have got a voluntary job with local charity shop
17.0 Get home and phone Josh and Millie[1]
18.0 Make some supper

Shit…know this will not work. Jane said that the children were going to be at after school club because she has started a job.

Shit… depression seeps in.
Why am I not there with them.
Another panic attack – I seem to slip into another dimension. It is always the same fleeting vision of being in a church, purple robes, suffocation and panic.
Feel ANGRY. HATE … is that enough fucking feeling?

[1] Patrick's children (pseudonyms)

29.4.09

Dear diary,
Shared these riveting entries with Sue – she made encouraging noises, "why does writing with the purple pen make you so angry" she asks. Stupid cow. Going down the gym.

p.s. Hate and Anger not really about purple pen – about being in that place. Suffocated by purple cloth and incense.

30.4.09

Dear diary,
A story came to me in the night:
Once upon a time there was a young boy. A saint in the making. His face shone with innocence and joy. Everything he touched turned into the colours of the rainbow. Each night however when he went home the light and joy and colour were sucked out of him by a large vampire bat that hung in the corner of his home. It had the face of the Devil. It never moved or spoke, just hung there in brooding silence.

His mother was a very holy woman and tried to keep him joyful, "leave him be" she said of the bat. "He's not hurting you. He doesn't really exist at all". Every day she went to the church to say her prayers and collect a bag full of blessings for the boy. So the boy went about his life and ignored the bat as best he could his face shining with joy.

The bat travelled with him in his heart however. It lay alongside the blessings until one day it spread its' wings and said, "I'm going to devour you". The boy asked "Why? I've always just let you be". The bat just grinned "that's my secret" and he ate away the boy's soul taking all the joy, the brightness from the boy's world.

I was reading some of G.K. Chesterton's writing today and came across this line:

> "I caught him with an unseen hook and an invisible line which is long enough to let him wander to the ends of the world, and still to bring him back with a twitch upon the thread" (Chesterton 1996).

Although Chesterton was alluding to God twitching the thread – it feels sometimes as if it is something totally evil that twitches me back and that God (if he exists) is powerless to intervene.

7.5.09

Still having nightmares, and they have spread to waking moments. I suddenly find myself shaking, terrified without reason. Something simple like a glimpse of a face half known, a smell of perfume, a purple cloth and I can feel my pulse racing I feel sick and want to run. It happened the other day in the local supermarket. I couldn't go through the till. I had to abandon my trolley half way down the aisle. Perhaps I am going mad.

Sue asked me if I had ever experienced these kind of feelings when I was a small child, but I haven't. I think that perhaps she thinks there is some kind of "abuse" in my history, but I really had a very ordinary childhood. My parents were ok – well my dad used to get depressed, but nothing out of the ordinary. I keep coming back to his face on the day of my ordination though. Not sure why.

18.05.09

I decided to take the bull by the horn and talk to my parents about my childhood to see if there is anything I should know about. Nothing out of the ordinary – apart from my Grandfather dying which I guess is normal and was not distressing to me. He was after all in his 80's and I had only met him two or three times.

Talking to my dad however I realised that he had been more depressed than I realised. I asked him about his tears when I was ordained and he made some lame excuse and changed the subject. That I thought was the end of the matter, but a few days later I received a letter from him – I can't ever remember receiving a letter from him so when I saw his writing on the envelope I felt quite sick and really anxious.

> Dear Patrick,
>
> I am sorry that I couldn't answer your questions when we met. I realise that you deserve some answers though; I thought if I wrote down some of the facts, you would know, and then if you want to talk to me about it later on, then we can do that. It is just really hard for me to say these things after all these years because of the shame and guilt I feel.

When I was a small child my parents used to take me to church. The priest was a friendly fellow and made a good deal of fuss of all the children. He used to organise a boy's club and take us out walking and visiting interesting places. We used to meet on a Tuesday evening. Some of the boys were promoted to "helper" status and would arrive early to set things up for the group, and stay afterwards to clear up. It was a position that carried great prestige (both with the other boys but also with the parents). What I discovered however was that it also carried tasks that related to relieving the sexual desire of the priest. We were bound by secrecy. What happened we were told was because we were bad. God would punish us if we spoke to anyone and we would never be forgiven. I still feel fear writing this, even knowing logically that this was nothing to do with God (and I do not believe in him now) but was more about the needs of a sick pervert.

I remember the first time it happened. I was so scared. I was sick afterwards and then walked home. Mum was so full of the priest's praise. I made myself keep going until I was 11 and then refused to have anything more to do with church. My mother and father were very upset, especially my father, who told me I would be damned to hell in the life to come, and perhaps I am.

When I married your mother I thought I could finally put all of this behind me, and largely I did, but the depression dogged me. Sometimes it has felt as if I am already in hell and cannot ever find my way out.

Having you was a miracle – and I really tried to support all of your choices, but when you chose the church, even though it was a different denomination, it felt like you were siding with that priest over me and your mother. It felt like being abused all over again.

I am sorry that I have not been able to be the father you want me to be, or that I have wanted to be. I guess from what you said the other day you are also fighting your own demons. We can talk about this when we next meet if you really want to, but I would rather just forget all about what happened then as they are memories I want to forget about. Your mum does know though; I did tell her the basic gist of what happened when we were first married.

It feels a bit strange writing a letter to you – but somehow it is easier to distance myself from those terrible times by writing rather than telling you face to face and seeing – I don't know, disgust, disappointment on your face.

Your loving father

25.5.09

I am not really sure what to do. The world feels as if it is slipping away from me. I re-read the letter several times. Suddenly things start to make a lot of sense and I realise why my father has always been ambivalent of my vocation as a priest. I realise that it is not about me though. I had always thought that he never thought I was good enough, that I had let him down in some way, or I was not suitable to be a priest and that was a failing on my part. However hard I tried to prove to him I was worthy, I failed. I recognise now though that it was never about me, it was about him, and how hurt he had been.

I met up with him in a pub last week and we talked a bit. He obviously finds all of this really hard to speak of. I even suggested that he had some counselling. What really gets me is the senselessness of it. Why would someone want to take pleasure out of having sex with a young child. It does not make any sense to me at all. It makes me feel physically sick.

27.5.09

The nightmares have been coming with vengeance. They seem to be worse since speaking to dad. Sometimes they happen in broad daylight. I am suddenly transported to another place another time. I feel overwhelming anxiety and fear. I start to shake and my legs turn to jelly. All I can see are fragmented images. Purple cloth; the smell of incense and sweat; a frighteningly huge penis thrust against my face; the feeling and taste of vomit on my lips. If they were not so upsetting they would be bizarre. I have never even really seen another man's penis, except perhaps in very innocent encounters in communal changing areas etc. When I described what was happening to Sue she said they sounded like what other people have described as "flashbacks". But how can I be having flashbacks about something that happened to my father? None of this makes any sense.

12.6.09

A lot has happened since my last entry. At Sue's suggestion my father came with me to one of my counselling sessions. It was quite an amazing hour. I talked about the experiences I was getting, and my depression. For the first time ever he talked about what happened to him when he was a child. The most bizarre thing was that what I was experiencing, and seeing, had actually happened to him. He had tried over the years to blot it out, but it had never gone. When I was a child he apparently often had major flashbacks and panic attacks. He described that when I was about four my mother left us together whilst she had to go to a hospital appointment in the nearby town. He became terrified that he was going to abuse me. Why I cannot imagine, he was one of the most gentle and respectful people I know. Apparently he often had these obsessive thoughts that terrified him. He said that he took me up to my bedroom and locked me in (so he was on the outside). He knew then that I would be safe. When he felt calmer he unlocked the door, but to his horror I was sitting on the floor cutting out bits from the illustrated bible that was in my room. I guess I got bored! The bit I apparently handed him was a section of the Ten Commandments. “You shall not commit adultery”. Obviously to me a child it meant nothing, but to him apparently it was a sign that he would never be forgiven for what had happened. For some reason he thought that the abuse was his fault. How does that work?

Talking about this with Sue we managed to piece together something of what had happened to him and make sense of it. In talking about it he has come to a realisation that as a small child this was not his fault. It was the fault of the priest. It was not God’s will. We will never know why the priest did it, perhaps just because he could. Sue gave him some contact details for some therapists and agencies that may be able to support him as he tries to make sense of his life.

I also need to go on to try to make sense of my own life. For reasons I cannot quite understand I feel deeply ashamed of my own role as a priest. I am truly shocked that a man set aside by God should violate trust in this way. It makes me doubt everything; even God’s existence; especially God’s existence.

29.7.09

I couldn’t bring myself to go to church at all last month. I do however feel better in some respects. I have not had any of the awful flashback/panic attacks that were leaving me so debilitated. I do however feel cut off, isolated, unable to re-connect with who I was, with my life as a priest. I cannot even bear to contemplate God. Is there a God? Sometimes I hope that there is not. What would a God who permitted this to happen be like? At other times I hope he does exist, just so that I can rage at him!

18.8.09

It was lovely to see my parents last week. They both seemed to have turned a corner and are happily engaged in doing the normal things of their lives, gardening, cooking; travelling about in their little camper van. My dad has joined a group for survivors of abuse within the Catholic Church and is receiving quite a bit of support. He has even been to church with my mum once or twice. He seems to smile a lot, something I realise was missing in the past.

The strange thing is that my father seems to have let go of all his anger with the Church and God, and I am really pleased about that, yet at the same time I am so angry. I seem to have inherited his anger, his hatred of everything clerical, just as I did his flashbacks. That sounds really crazy; perhaps I am losing my grip on sanity! I still feel deeply hurt and angry. I am not sure that I will ever go back to where I was. Sue has suggested that perhaps I see a spiritual director, but I think that I prefer just to talk things through with her. Trusting someone from the clergy, even though I know in my heart many are wonderful men and women; many in fact are my friends, will take time.

25.9.09

Something has changed. I am not sure when or how, but I do feel very different. I can sometimes go several days without feeling angry!! I think that I have written myself into a different place. I have been studying the bible, the Quran and the Torah, looking at God's interaction with the world, and written long commentaries on how the scripture relates to God's relationship with me. Sue looked a bit glum when I suggested she read it! I can begin to see a new relationship with God emerging. Before my understandings were based on assumptions that were not true (both about me and the world) and now I recognise that I cannot make assumptions about anything, some things I will never completely "know" they will remain mysteries and that is ok.

I have also just enrolled with the local university to do a foundation degree course in counselling. Having seen how it works in action I think that this is perhaps something that I can do, and be quite good at! Sue is very supportive. I still see her for occasional top up sessions.

18.6.10

I received a letter last week from my counsellor Sue. She is planning a book looking at sexual abuse and how it affects the wider family. She has asked me if I would like to be one of the contributor's. I did not even have to think about it, my answer was YES! YES!

3.11.10

I met again with Sue last week and we talked more about the book. We have been talking about how we might like to work together on this. I feel quite excited, and I realise that finally I am beginning to re-join the human race. I think, for my parent's sake, I will write anonymously this will also give me the freedom from the secrets.

CHAPTER EIGHT

WORKING WITH ELSA IN ORDER TO "ESCAPE THE GRIP" OF A RELIGIOUS CULT

Elsa self-referred in 2002 to a community based counselling service where I was working. The counselling service operated alongside a drop-in centre that supported people with mental health difficulties. She was 24 and really struggling to come to terms with her recent departure from a religious community where she had lived all her life with her parents and brothers. She felt very strongly that leaving was, "the right thing to do" but found it very difficult now to adjust to living outside the community and without any contact with her family. She was in the care of the local mental health team and had recently been given a diagnosis for schizophrenia. Because she felt, "so fragile…sometimes I feel s if I am going to fall into a million pieces if a breeze comes on me" her CPN[1] (who we have called Diane) attended counselling sessions with her to give her some support and to ensure she felt safe. This was good because it enabled Elsa to tell her story, and have it witnessed by someone compassionate, and through Diane's understanding of her story, helped her link more successfully with the mental health team and the services they offered.

When I moved to a different area I lost touch with Elsa, but she contacted me by email in 2011 following the publication of my book, "Where Angels Fear to Tread" (Dale 2010) which had been lent to her by a friend. She told me that the stories had really resonated with her and wondered whether she could also find some way of talking about her life so that, "others can find some hope". She has often thought about writing but has not felt able to write under her own name for fear of reprisals against her family who are still involved with the community. We wondered how we could write in ways that "spoke out about these

[1] Community Psychiatric Nurse

unspeakable things" yet kept her, and others safe. I also wondered how we could write about our conversations when they had taken place in a setting outside my private practice, in an agency that is no longer in existence, and that involved a third party, Diane who we had both lost contact with. I was also concerned whether talking about these issues would take Elsa back into very difficult thoughts and feelings which I would not be able to support her with (we now live to far apart to meet).

What emerged through our email conversations was that there was more than one story to tell and that the newest story which was as Elsa said, "full of hope and change and so different from the history of me". We wondered whether there was perhaps a way that she could tell this story to the little girl she described as being inside her who had, "lost her mind, her soul and her family". This she felt would help her to, "re-write who I am". Elsa decided to write her story with the help of her support worker Anne (who helps her with some of the tasks she still feels challenging). What interested, and surprised me, was that alongside Elsa's story, which was sent to me by email, Anne had also written her reactions in the form of an email commentary. She commented on what surprised her, and resonated with her as she typed Elsa's words, and she copied these comments to Elsa. As I read the emerging stories I could sense that Elsa's original writings and experiences of herself was changing as a result of Anne's words. The effect was similar to that I have seen in the narrative therapy practice of "outsider witness or definitional ceremony" (White 2003:165-219); where a person's story is witnessed by others, not in terms of giving praise or criticism, but more with a view to the witness allowing the stories to resonate with their own life experiences, and re-telling the story in terms of their own life experiences; commenting on what images, feelings and memories of their own the stories evoked[2]. The original story teller having heard the witnesses account then responds and usually the telling of their story has been enriched by the experience of the witness. It was originally used by Myerhoff (1979; 1986; 1982), an anthropologist to re-connect members of an elderly Jewish community who were losing their connections with each other and their cultural identity. Narrative therapists commonly use these practices to enable people who feel isolated in their experiences to re-connect with others and develop a richer sense of self (White 2000). For readers interested in definitional ceremony and outsider witness practices I have given a fuller description in earlier

[2] For more information on definitional ceremony see White (2003)

writing[3]. Also excellent guidelines for those participating in such ceremonies and practices are given by White (2003).

With both Elsa and Anne's permission both the story and the email conversations have been included so that the reader can gain understanding of this process. The stories emerging are not; problem or trauma saturated. They start with the transmission of trauma across the generations; but immerge as new stories of hope and resilience and as Elsa comments, "new beginnings".

Elsa on Escaping the Grip of the community

The Church of the Kingdom, as I shall call it, was not just a place you went to on a Sunday, but a community where we lived, worked and prayed together. I didn't join it; I was born into it. My mother joined it as a young teenager. I have no other memories of living anywhere else as a child. One of my first memories was of the chapel. It was a dark austere place tucked away in the basement of the large Victorian house that was our home. The memories are of my mother on her knees scrubbing the floor, and on Sundays; long services where the minister shouted and stood tall above us. The walls were lined with gloomy pictures and grim sayings such as, "the wages of sin are death". We just sat, knelt or stood for what seemed like hours listening to his voice, sometimes we sang. I liked singing. At least that was a happy sound. There didn't seem to be much joy, or compassion, or even God, in that chapel; just finger pointing and fear. The children of the community came here for their lessons. There were about a dozen of us ranging in ages from 5 to 16. Boys were taught separately after the age of 11 as it was considered unseemly for us to be together after that age.

There was a lot of fear. Fear of getting it wrong. Fear of going to hell. Fear of losing my mum. Even as a small child I knew she was so unhappy. She used to cut her arms sometimes. Something she was publicly punished for; if anyone noticed, which is why she always wore long sleeves. I never knew my father. He was an elder in the church and had, I learned later, fallen out of favour with the minister and been expelled. We were kept in the community under sufferance and under protection of the minister. Everything, every scrap of food, every piece of clothing was given to us by others and we had to be grateful. So grateful all the time, and always treated like second class citizens.

I remember one particular elder Colin, who my mother was always afraid of. He was a bully and I think now he probably forced her to have

[3] See Dale (2010; 2011)

sex with him, but at the time, as a child, all I was aware of was that she was afraid of him. He used to sometimes grip her shoulder and say, “you are a sinner who needs to repent”. She spent hours each day on her knees praying. Colin’s wife was often ill, she had one little boy who was about six months younger than me, and I remember her being pregnant several times, but there were never any more babies. The community believed in the power of prayer, not in hospitals or doctors. If you were ill it was because of sin.

The word, “repentance” was one of the first words I learnt to spell. We were home educated so that we would not be corrupted by the wickedness of others. I remember going to the shop (a rare treat) and seeing other children with their parents. They wore bright colours; chatting and playing together with no cares in the world. We were told never to look at others but just to focus on what we were doing. Never to talk to outsiders about what went on in the community. Those living outside the community we were told, “are sinful and will be brought to the terrible judgement”. I remember secretly looking at these children and their parents on our rare outings and thinking that they didn’t look or act particularly sinfully.

When I was ten my mother married again; another member of the community; I don’t even know if she divorced my dad, or was even married to him, but in the communities eyes he was dead, so she married again. My mother never seemed happy, always fearful, but as my brother was born about eight months later I guess she didn’t have too many choices. Twelve months after that my youngest brother arrived. Some things improved. Our standing in the community, now that we had a father, was better. We all had better clothes and my step-father was quite a kind man. I just loved my small brothers and was often the person who they ran to when they wanted something. Parents were not supposed to cuddle their children, but as a sister I could tuck them into bed and give them a big hug. It was probably the only time I remember hugging anyone all the time I was growing up.

My mother was so unhappy, I could tell that. She wouldn’t talk to me about it, even when I asked. She often sat in an upright chair rocking it as if it had rockers. It creaked, and as it creaked she would read out loud from the scriptures. Her favourite texts were either the book of Job or Revelation. The terror of the latter battling the depression of the first. The words, familiar, terrified me. Who was this God we were worshipping to bring all this grief? When I was fifteen my mother died. I am not sure, even now, what happened. I think she probably killed herself. I know there was a huge upset in the community and we were told to pray for redemption for her sins. I remember outsiders coming into the community room, but we were not told who they were or what they wanted. There was a funeral service in the chapel, but she was buried outside in a service attended by just the men. My step-father retreated into his own world, and my brothers by this time were being educated by the men were not able to spend much time with me. I by this time was sharing a room with three other teenage girls (all sisters) who didn't really talk to me. It was a lonely time, I was so unhappy. I thought often about escape, both in running away, and of ending my life, but I was so scared of the consequences. When you have been told from a young age about eternal damnation and the evilness of the outside world it is very hard to contemplate not doing as you are told.

I guess that is when Pip came into my life. He was like my guardian angel, someone I could talk to and who loved me. No-one else could see him he was like my daemon (a guardian spirit). The community would have been outraged had they known, and in fact when I was even caught talking to myself, there was a whole evening of laying on of hands to cast out the devil. I wondered sometimes whether Pip was the devil, but he didn't seem to have the tell tale signs, and although I felt guilty, I couldn't give him up – he was just there for me. He kept me sane. Eventually (I was eighteen) we decided that we had to leave. The minister and elders were considering marrying me to one of the older men. I was just terrified. There was something about the way this man looked at me that was terrifying. It was even more terrifying than the thought of leaving. So one day I just walked into the garden and walked out. I didn't really have a plan, I didn't know much about the outside world. I knew nothing really. Just walked out, and wandered through the streets. I carried nothing with me apart from my bible, and within me Pip. I wandered for such a long time. I'm still not really sure what happened in those days, weeks and months that followed. Sometimes I remember glimpses of faces in my nightmares, sometimes a smell, sweet and sickly, a feeling of floating and also pain.

I ended up in hospital. They said I had overdosed on heroin. That was the beginning of my life now. This is where I live now. The community never tried to contact me, I knew they wouldn't. Once you are out you are on your own without God's grace for ever. There is no going back. It is about free will. And my will <u>is</u> free now, and I am grateful. I just have Pip, but even in this outside world he is not really approved of, and medicated against. But there are other people who I count as friends and on the whole my life is ok. I cry for my mother and my brothers sometimes, but there is nothing I can do. My brothers would not be able to contact me now; if they did they would be outcasts too.

Email Conversations with Anne - Elsa's Support Worker

Dear Sue,

I have attached Elsa's story.

I have known her for three years, and never ever guessed about her early life. I am quite amazed and wanted to share some of this amazement before it gets lost in every day doings.

I am so amazed that she had the courage and strength to leave the community. It must have been a terrifying, and to leave her brothers must have been so hard. The phrase she uses, "my will is free now" keeps coming back to me, and brings tears to my eyes. I hadn't realised either how important a part Pip has played in her life. I had known about him, and about her diagnosis for schizophrenia, which I had always thought was a bad thing, and something to be avoided. But her saying, "he has kept me sane" has made me really re-think all my training and thinking about mental illness and how we work with those who have another person living in their head.

I get very angry when I hear about religious groups that bully people. I think this tie in with my own experiences of growing up as a "good Catholic girl". So much guilt and shame that I was never going to be good enough. Fear that I would be condemned to hell for committing so many transgressions. As I typed Elsa's words I also thought about my own mum who was so unhappy, but unwaveringly catholic until her death five years ago.

I remember standing crying by her grave at the funeral and thinking, "Why couldn't she just love me? Why couldn't she love me more than the rules of this faith? Why has she left me alone?" I have never found answers. Perhaps with time however acceptance has come and the knowledge that in her own way, despite everything, she tried her best to love me. I remember when I was about 15 and throwing a wobbly about something and she just put her arms around me and said, "what ever you do, remember I love you". I wonder whether Elsa's mum was ever able to show, even in a small way that she loved her?

Elsa talking about these things has really brought it home to me how important having a free will is, and that even people who don't seem to have any choices can sometimes find freedom.

Dear Anne,

Thank you so much for this, and indeed for your own comments. I wonder how you would feel about sharing these comments also with Elsa. What you have said, your own questions about religion and the impact Elsa's story has had on you will I think be of interest to her.

Dear Sue,

I've thought about this quite a lot, and I think I would be really happy to share my comments with Elsa. She has been incredibly courageous about talking about things that she had always been told to keep secret. I think I need some courage to, to stand alongside and speak out too.

Elsa Joins the Conversation

Dear Sue and Anne,

I was so touched by both Anne and Sue's comments. It is difficult to put into words what it means that someone has listened to my life story and said that it has meant something to them. Anne's comments about her own mother and her feelings when she died made me want to rage with her and in some strange way that made me feel stronger. For the first time she was not just someone who did her job with me (very well), but a real person who I could relate to.

I'm not sure I ever really knew my mother. She kept her grief from me, and as much as possible protected me from what was going on in the community. In the past I (like Anne) have always raged at her for not loving me enough, for putting the community first, but reading this and thinking about it I guess what I have been wondering is whether her keeping her grief from me was in fact a gift. The only gift she could give in a really tough place.

I was never physically or sexually abused while I was at the community. Lots of psychiatrists have asked me that question, and not really believed me when I have said no. But no-one tried to have sex with me, which they did with some of the girls who were without fathers. You may think that this was a good thing, and I guess it was, but at the time this felt terrible, as if I was so terrible no-one would want me. It seems a secret far worse than being able to say "yes I was abused", because if I had been then I would have a reason to hate them. I was one of the lucky ones however. My mother stood between me and what might have been and I hated her for it and that causes me shame too. I know for a fact however that she was sexually abused by several of the men in the community.

When I talked to Anne the other day she said that, "shame is a real bugger" which made me laugh. The laughter between us made the shame slightly easier to bear. She also asked me how I managed to have the courage to come out of the community.

I guess I felt it was the only answer. Staying felt like dying, and I really wanted to live. Coming out of the community was just too much though. When you have been told over and over again that outside is evil; that is what you find, evil. Everything you thought you knew about your world, even if that world was a crappy one, suddenly feels safe compared to what was going on outside. I'm not sure I'm ready to think about that yet, or whether I will ever be. All I can say is that I think I finally found out what it was like to live the life of my mother. To have other people demanding sex from you; to have no power over anything. But unlike her I did not die, but walked away and I am living proof that it can be done!

Dear Elsa,

It was so good that you felt able to write, and also that Anne's comments were helpful and that you felt, "listened to".

I was (and still am) amazed by your courage firstly in walking away from the community, and then secondly walking away from the life you found when you left the community. Walking away once must have been hard, but walking away twice was doubly amazing. I wonder where that courage came from? Was there was anyone in your life who had demonstrated this kind of courage, or whether it was something about you and your values and hopes and beliefs about things?

Anne is right shame is a right bugger. Shame is also (as you have found) a laughable figure. Laughing together with Anne loosened his/her grip on you. What other things is s/he afraid of do you think?

Dear Sue,

I laughed when I got your email. It was the kind of questions you used to ask me when we met together for our counselling.

I think the courage was something firstly I learnt from my Mum. She had it in a different way in that she had the courage never to tell me about how awful she was feeling. Secondly I think one of the older women in the community showed me that whatever happens to your body (she was often beaten for being outspoken by the elders) you can believe your own thoughts and think your own dreams. Also, I think that for me, I never thought about it as courage; but more about being true to my own thoughts and feelings and this being true means I am alive. Without it I am nothing.

On the second question. Shame is definitely a "HE". He is born out of the attitude of the elders who always looked down their noses at women, made them feel small, that to be looked on with desire by one of them was all that was important in life. I have decided not to live with him; "SHAME" any more. He is defunct in my life, and that feels very good. If I feel him creeping up on me I shall laugh in his face!

I still talk to Anne and show her what I have written. It is strange because I didn't think I would be able to write about myself (which is why I asked her to help me) but now I have started I find I can. Anne says she is a great supporter standing on the sidelines with a football rattle.

Dear Elsa,

Yes. You can indeed write for your self; and that is great! Have you got any other supporters standing on the sidelines I wonder?

So glad to hear that SHAME is not living with you any more, and that you have some weapons of mass destruction e.g. laughter, if he dares to show his face again. What is that like, I wonder, to live without him interfering?

Being alive seems very important to you, even when you have found yourself in really, really, difficult situations. I know what being alive means to me, but I am wondering what it means to you?

Dear Sue,

Being alive is the sun on my face; the birds singing in the trees; the spiritual connection with me, and the world around me. Standing on the beach with the sound of the sea pounding against the pebbles; the wind whipping my hair I find the freedom to reach out and touch the edges of the universe.

Being alive is having a free will. Then I am able to make choices for myself; eating what I want to eat, thinking my own thoughts and it not mattering what other people think.

Being alive is dancing with Pip in the moonlight and not caring if people think I'm mad.

The opposite of that is the kind of life I had in the community. If death is like that, I do not want to die!

You asked me if I had any other supporters – that made me smile. The thought of the people around me carrying football rattles and scarves and screaming for me at the top of their lungs. But yes when I think of it there are lots of folks both who know me well, and who know me a little who stand on the sidelines of my life and cheer me on.

Anne of course – she is a really hero, helping me with all those annoying things that I still find hard to do for myself. I suppose my psychiatrist Dr. (Name deleted) although he would look a bit strange dressed as a football supporter! Although he is a bit scary and sometimes challenges the, "free will bit" he has never given up on me. There is Max the caretaker at the flats, he always has a cheery word and helps me sometimes when I can't find my keys or have too much shopping. There are the girls at the bingo, they always make me laugh when I can't find the numbers on the card. There is Christabelle (my cat) who is a bit choosy about her food, but always rubs round my legs in the mornings. There is of course Pip. Although other people are rather scared of him. I know him. He is a me that is truly free. There is my friend Rick – although small doses of him (because he talks such a lot). There is even my mum, although she died a long time ago. She is around me and I can feel her presence. There is the choir that I recently joined. Growing up in a place where singing was part of everyday life has been an advantage. People there don't ask me much about me (which is a great relief) but we are kind of united in a purpose. Making music together and that is great.

Sorry Sue – that sounds a bit like an epic team of supporters (and yes you are one too). I giggle when I think of them all together. I hadn't really thought about how many people are actually parts of my life. I have always thought of myself as a bit of a loner.

Dear Elsa,

Wow! An epic team indeed. What is it like to know that all these folks are part of your world?

So glad to hear that your Mum is also part of this team. Do you think she would have anything to say about all of this?

Dear Sue,

Yes I think she would feel that she had in some way done something for me, and that this had lessened the hold the community had over her.

I think also of my brothers sometimes, and hope that one day they will be able to feel free to. I know now though that this has to be their choice. Just as I had a choice, they will too and I know that however much I want to, I cannot rescue them.

I feel very different from that scared thing that came to see you for some counselling. As I write I can hear the winter wind in the trees over the road and I know I am free. Even Dr (name deleted) thinks I am doing ok. He has reduced my medication a bit, and actually smiled at me! I never thought that day would come.

I am happy for you to include any or all of this in your book (if you think it is worth it) but think you will have to change the names as although I am not ashamed (don't do that any more) of what I have said I don't want people to judge me just by these words. I want the freedom to be who I want to be. Hope that is ok.

Dear Elsa,

Of course that is ok. Your story is definitely worth telling. It gives people hope that they can have the courage to walk away from the most difficult situations, and that there is a life which is full of freedom, hope and people who care about them.

To conclude this chapter I thought that it may be helpful to reflect on these conversations above in terms of the practice of narrative therapy and narrative research. Although these conversations did not take place with the explicit intention of being therapeutic, we were in fact intending to co-research the experiences of Elsa in respect of her relationships with trauma, the religious community which she had grown up in. As we started to write together however what in fact seemed more important, was to engage with Elsa in ways that empowered and enabled her to move beyond being described in terms of trauma and mental illness. Having already had a history of meeting with Elsa in a therapeutic setting I considered that I needed to put her needs before the needs of any research venture I might have in mind. Making ethical decisions and gaining informed consent when undertaking this kind of project is never a once and only signature on a piece of paper (Josselson, Lieblich, and McAdams 2003); it is more a dynamic part of the research process that has to constantly be re-visited and re-evaluated in light of the emerging data (Bond 2004). Having had a pre-existing relationship with Elsa, meant that I had to accept responsibility for ensuring that her needs were met rather than my own. What emerged through our conversations became an extension of the therapeutic process (Etherington 2001). I consider that despite the conversations taking a different from anticipated form they also gave a unique insight into the transmission of trauma across the generations.

As others before me have pointed out (White 2000; Speedy 2007, 2004) having conversations with others about their life experiences will change both the experience of both the teller and the listener. Gathering life stories is not a process that leaves no trace. As stated before there is certainly evidence to suggest that using witnesses to resonate and reflect back to a person (who is telling a story of their life) in terms of what they have heard, and the stories of their own lives this telling has evoked, does indeed re-connect people with others across a shared theme. White says of his own work where this happens and gives examples. He says:

> "Definitional Ceremonies provided an antidote to the effects of the isolation experienced by the people of this community and the sense of invisibility that was a chief outcome of this isolation" (White 2007:181).

Although my writing with Elsa and Anne has not constituted a formal definitional ceremony in the sense that White speaks of, I consider that the effects of Anne reflecting back to Elsa with the inclusion of her own story did change Anne's experience, and she started to tell different less isolated stories of her experiences.

It is common Narrative Therapy practice to have "re-membering conversations" (White 2007) such that the person, who often feels isolated, re-connects with significant others who have been part of their life story in positive ways. It also gives opportunity for them to review their relationship with those people, or even feelings, that are not so positive. They are effectively moving from positions of isolation to being a part, and a member, of a community. For example, Elsa re-members her life with "supporters"; people from both the past and the present who she sees as significant in supporting her, and standing alongside her, as she renegotiates her relationship with SHAME. This way of working is taken from the work of anthropologist Myerhoff who says:

> "Re-membering, then, is a purposive, significant unification, quite different from the passive, continuous fragmentary flickerings of images and feelings that accompany other activities in the normal flow of consciousness" (Myerhoff 1982:111)

Re-membering, as White goes on to say, "Contributes to the development of a 'multivoiced' sense of identity and facilitates activity in making sense of one's existence"(White 2007:136). Within my emails to Elsa I tried to help her reconnect with those people in her life who had sustained her and I just loved the image of a group of football supporters cheering her on from the sidelines. Hopefully it is evident that this was of benefit to her, and the light heartedness belies the serious attempt to challenge the situations and people who were isolating and disempowering her.

Part III

Conflict and War

CHAPTER NINE

A BROTHER AND SISTER'S STORY: USING A "LIFE STORY" APPROACH

Sajela and Orthie contacted me at the beginning of 2010 on the recommendation of their therapist, who had been involved in a previous narrative research project with me. They wanted to find ways of telling their stories to audiences such that the conflict in the Democratic Republic of Congo was highlighted, and also the plight of refugees fleeing from conflict. They also hoped that being enabled to "write" their story would help them, "make some sense out of what had happened to them and their families". On meeting with them we talked about how this process might happen, and indeed explored possibilities of them writing a book in their own names. This seemed at the moment to be too big a step, and they preferred to be involved in the researching, and writing of, a section of this book concerning the intergenerational effects of childhood trauma. They also wanted to continue to work with my colleague in a therapeutic relationship, and use this if necessary to support them through this writing process. They have adopted pseudonyms to protect their identity, and the identity of other family members.

As Orthie was only fifteen at the time of our meeting and I was aware that I needed to ensure, because of his age, that he had a clear understanding of what he was asking to be part of, and that his parents, therapist and others would support his decision to be engaged in this process. He was, after all, not yet considered "an adult" in the eyes of the law. Following much discussion between Orthie, his mum; sister, therapist and myself we all concluded that this was something he was able, and willing to consent to. I was also aware that the other contributor's were much older, and I wondered whether this would affect them, or the process. It is interesting however that at the end of this writing and researching it was felt by all of us that he was an important member of the group. As Patrick comments, "he is a vital member of our team. He is the next generation, the reason we are all working so hard on all of this. What he has shared and given has been life-changing".

I feel that since meeting Sajela and Orthie I have been on a steep learning curve. Whereas most of the writing I do is with people who are exploring issues that I have either personal, or professional, knowledge about; this felt very different. To my shame I knew very little about the conflict in the Democratic Republic of Congo, and little about the experiences of asylum seekers in this country. What I have learnt has shocked me. I am sure that I have not done justice to the enormity of what is happening to millions of people in a country far away from the UK, but I hope in sharing the life stories of two remarkable people it will at least start to break the silence and open discussion on issues of human rights within both countries.

This chapter hopes to act as an introduction to Sajela and Orthie, but firstly just a few words about "life story" research.

A life story approach

My normal approach towards narrative research is to see the writing of the narrative as socially constructing the reality of the person doing the writing. This means that the narratives may, but do not always, contain historic facts, and are not seen as describing "truths" that were there prior to the writing. Many however (Clandinin and Connelly 2000; French et al. 2007; Goodson 2001) use narrative research in a different way, and use narratives people tell them to collate facts and histories, in order to enable others to have an understanding of what has happened during the course of specific events and times. For example life story and oral history projects have brought the history of World War II to life for those of us to young to remember (Terkel 1997) and online resources such as Rutgers Oral History (2012) offer a data base of hundreds of personal accounts.

Because it seemed important both for myself, and readers, to gain an insight into something of the ongoing conflict in the Congo, and into the UK's asylum system life story writing felt a very good approach to use. In later chapters of the book Sajela and Orthie, alongside other contributors, use narratives within a collective narrative to socially construct realities. What follows next is Sajela's written account of her memories of leaving the Congo:

Sajela: Early memories of my home

I was born in 1984 in what was then called, Zaire; but has now become the Democratic Republic of Congo in a small village about twenty miles or so from Kisangani close to the Congo river. I lived with my mother, and Uncle's family. I never knew my father as he had died before my birth. My memories of that place are fragmentary images; hot, muddy, potholed tracks, the forest to the edge of our village; damp and dark. The smells: sometimes of spice sometimes of sewage; the sounds of laughter coming from children playing in an old ruined house. Singing women; brightly dressed. Once I remember going into Kisangani, walking for what seemed to me, a small child, a lifetime, through shack like hamlets towards what to all appearances was a western style town. Modern buildings and people selling all sorts of goods; no electricity or wages though, and little running water though!

I remember hunger. Not, the sort of peckish feeling that British people describe when waiting for a meal, but a day after day gnawing pain of not enough anywhere to alleviate that pain. This is not because the country suffers the droughts other African countries have. We have a tropical monsoon climate with high humidity and lush pastures and forest. Hunger comes however from war and chaos taking away our food sources. Animals killed, crops wrecked, sometimes no-one to tend or sow them. Sometimes there was flooding, but not in my memory.

My family were Christian. Not the kind of hymn singing agnostics you find in the UK, but more a kind of desperate faith mixed up with local customs and traditions. It was called the Église de Jésus-Christ sur Terre par le Prophète Simon Kimbangu—EJCSK. In the time of colonization by the Belgians it was an outlawed church, but it has some legal recognition.[1]

My country, in my experience, has always been torn by war and the greed for power of man over man. Ethnic tensions, one group of people trying to show their dominance over another; I never discovered why. In 1996 there was a revolution. As a child at the time, I did not really understand, and it is still hard to make sense of, but I think that it was when Kabila wrested power from the despot Sese Seko. Refugees and warriors alike poured over the borders from neighbouring Rwanda where there had been genocide of the kind that even the world had taken note of. The new regime was also inept, further war erupted and since then so many conflicts, each with greedy men trying to take charge by way of violence. The men; and even young boys were taken into the armies to fight. The women chattels despoiled by capturing armies. The DRC is home to over

[1] Church of Jesus Christ on Earth by the Prophet Simon Kimbangu

fifty million people and the size of Western Europe. It is not a simple conflict to understand, especially for outsiders. There are over fifteen rebel groups and armies from many countries. There is strand upon strand of complexity. As the Congolese saying goes "power is eaten whole because power eats whole".

Violence came to our village in 1996. It was a hot night; the rains had not come, everywhere was shimmering with heat. The black clouds sent spirals of flies onto the remaining livestock. All I remember from that night was being bundled with the other children out into the forest, into what you would probably call a hut. We were locked in and told to be quiet and still. The small children cried for their mothers. We heard the sounds of weapons, shouting, screaming; smelt the smoke of fire but still we hid. I think we were there for three days. It was hot airless, not easy to breathe. Our water ran out, so did the food and there were no latrines. Several small children developed a fever and two died, one of them in my arms. I was about eleven at the time. Eventually someone came for us.

What we returned to was desolation. Our village ransacked. Some of the men had been away from the village at the time; others who were there were killed. My mother and most of the women in the village had been brutally raped, some killed. It was (and still is) a political strategy that to despoil the women and plant seed in them will win the war (whatever that is about). My mother had three broken ribs, and had internal injuries which never healed. Her head had been shaved and she was pregnant with my brother. Other women had been even more brutally treated with limbs and breasts missing. One had been beheaded and left lying in the middle of the track. These were sights no child, or adult for that matter, should have to witness. What monsters had done this?

The men folk who were left buried the dead and rebuilt some shelters for us; this was very hard to do as so much of the landscape had been destroyed. All our livestock either perished or was taken captive. Buildings were burnt, and our water supply contaminated with some kind of oil. Trees had been hacked down. My mother never really recovered, she died in 1997 shortly after giving birth to Orthie. It was as if she gave up the will to live.

My uncle was a man of means, and thought well of within the community. He had been away when the ravagers had come. He and the other men decided that the girls and infants needed to flee our country of birth. He was afraid that the same fate would await us; as happened to our mothers. I remember him saying that the women were the only hope for our land. Plans were made, and after my mother died they came to fruition.

With the baby on my back and my cousins alongside we started a long journey out of my village. My uncle carried all that was our life on his back. I wept as I walked, then became so tired that even weeping seemed too much effort. We took lifts occasionally, when we could, at other times we walked. Sometimes sleeping in the open, at other times finding solace from villages on route. Eventually we walked, together with many others, into a refugee camp outside the city that is now called now Kinshasa. There were miles of tent like shacks made up of plastic and cloth, anything people could find to keep out the weather. People were dying of malnutrition, pneumonia and malaria. Two doctors from an international aid effort struggled against the overwhelming need of too many people and no provisions or facilities. Of our group of 16 from my village only my brother and I survived together with my Uncle and one other young woman. I read statistics on the Congo now and figures like 5.4 million killed since 1998 mean little unless you have witnessed the smell of death and dying, and witnessed the atrocities of raids on the villages.

We were the fortunate ones. My Uncle had some money so secured us a lift to the border with Angola. Everything within the Democratic Republic of Congo operates by way of bribes and mistrust. Everyone has an agenda, and it usually involves money changing hands, and even then often people are betrayed. We were tied into the back of jeeps under sacking, staying there for 5 days with just a few stops in the dark for water and dry bread. My baby brother sucked against my empty chest. There was nothing I could give him but single drops of water on my finger tips. Once we were stopped by militia, young boys carrying Kalashnikovs; I remember seeing them standing there, the guns nearly as tall as they were, and being so afraid; they did not speak our language; my Uncle however still had some money and he paid them off.

Over the border in Angola we were housed and fed by some families who had come earlier. It was so good to feel a little safe, and be somewhere that was not moving. After a couple of weeks we secured a place on a small boat travelling out of Angola headed for Spain; then we were to travel by road into France. Two days out however, the boat got into difficulties. There were too many of us, and the sea was too rough. It lurched and drew in water, the engine failing. One passenger fell overboard and was lost. Possessions were ditched in an attempt to keep afloat. It was terrifying. There were some life jackets; but not enough to go round.

I managed to keep hold of my brother, but all our possessions, little though they now were, went over with everything else. Some were praying but I did not even have the courage to pray. I could not imagine a God who had let such things happen caring about us. After a night of storm we were seen by a passing cargo vessel. They were headed, we learnt, for the UK. Big men heaved us over into first small motorised boats, then up onto the deck of a huge vessel. We learnt that we were way off course. Several days later we were picked up by coast guards and taken on board their vessel; eventually being deposited at a detention centre in the UK.

I still remember the feeling of, so much relief, at seeing this huge ship; we hoped so much that they would see us, even though we needed to travel unseen; but we were so desperate, and so small in the vast ocean. They fed us bread and some kind of cereals; they also found some milk for my brother and managed to make a feeder for him out of a plastic water bottle and the top of a rubber glove. The relief was overwhelming. The terror of what might happen next was as yet to materialise.

Orthie: Early memories

My only living blood relative that I know of is my sister. She has described to me our flight from Africa, but I do not remember anything before being in the UK, perhaps that is merciful. My Uncle I only remember fleetingly. He was I understand sent back to the Congo after a year of fighting for status as a refugee. We have not heard from him since.

I suppose I have always maintained my British status as being more important. I was after all very small when we came to Britain.

CHAPTER TEN

ASYLUM: FROM DETENTION TO CITIZENSHIP AND BEYOND

Within the UK there are currently twelve purpose defined immigration detention and removal centres for people entering the country illegally, including Tinsley House (located near Gatwick airport)[1] where Sajela and her Uncle were housed at the beginning of 1998 for nearly two years whilst they applied for asylum.

Tinsley House was newly built when they arrived and they were initially housed with other families. Because of Orthie's age, and when it was realised that Sajela was not his mother, he was placed under the care of the local authority and lived with a foster family. Although supervised visits were arranged it was hard for Sajela to maintain close contact with her brother. When in 2000 her Uncle was returned to the Democratic Republic of Congo Sajela aged 13 was also placed under the care of the local authority and was fostered (with a different family from her brother – who had by this time been accepted for adoption).

Orthie – Memories of the asylum centre

As I have said, I do not have any memories of our escape from the Congo, my earliest memories are of visiting my sister in the centre. Even then I don't have proper joined up thoughts about this. Just fragments of memory. My sister crying; barbed wire on the fences; an amazing play area with all sorts of toys and jigsaws; the smell of urine; cold grey skies; my sister holding me far too tight and me struggling to get free.

[1] For more details about this and other centres see web site: http://www .ukba.homeoffice.gov.uk/aboutus/organisation/immigrationremovalcentres

I used to go each week to see both her and my Uncle. I have no real memories of my Uncle, which makes me sad, but I do remember seeing my sister there, and not wanting to let her go at the end of our time together. Apparently I had to be distracted otherwise the whole thing would end in tears. It seems to me now sad that we couldn't have been kept together; we had after all been through so much. Surely filial bonds, and yes I think Sajela was a mother to me, should mean something? She had no choice when I was born, without her I would have died. Splitting us apart was a terrible thing to do.

Sajela: Memories of the detention centre

At first it was a relief to be somewhere safe, and we were together – our little family. All that was left. Then we were interviewed, over and over; the rooms were dim containing three or sometimes four plastic chairs and a table; a camera recording our every word. I always felt like a prisoner. Trapped. A translator was provided, but there were always locked doors and rooms I wanted to run from. We were after all prisoners.

They realised after the first or second interview that Orthie was not my son. As he was so small they removed him from my care and sent him out of the centre. They did explain to me that they wanted him to have the best possible care (he was of course only small) and that he could visit me; to me it felt like the end of the world. I had been his mother for so long and it felt like he was torn, literally, from my breast. There seemed nothing left for me or of me. I could not get to him. He came once a week with his new foster mother, and she sat whilst we were together. To start with he just clung to me and sobbed. They thought that he would probably settle better if he did not see me as often. So there was a gap of about one month (I crossed off the days on my calendar) and when he came next he seemed not to recognise me. He was well, but not my Orthie any more. He spoke in English to me. I felt my heart would break; but I still had a little hope. He was after all safe and well.

I went to school in the centre – I learnt to read and speak English; I loved the books, but I longed to see the countryside, the sky over the sea. I felt very cold, especially that first winter. This place was like one I had never been to before. Other people at the centre were kind to me, but they had their own troubles. The staff looking after us were largely indifferent. Some were better than others. I remember one worker who always stopped and talked to me, treated me like a person rather than a "thing", that made all the difference. Often families were split up, fathers ending up in one centre and mothers and children in others. The stories of their voyages were so sad. Often appeals would fail, and then the family would be whisked away. I assume they were sent back to wherever they came from. Then it was my Uncle's turn. The courts decided that he could be safely sent back to the Congo. He was, so they thought, at no risk. They decided because of what happened to our mother, we would stay in the UK (at least until we were 16). They also appointed us a guardian and a social worker. I remember my Uncle coming to say goodbye to me. He told me that he did not expect to see me again. I could not believe this was happening. From the day he left, until now, I have never heard from him. I assume he is dead.

Orthie – Growing up in South London

Growing up in South London seemed relatively easy. I had friends who went to the same school, other black boys and girls around and about. I knew that I was different; for one thing my adoptive mother was also black, but not as black as me. When I was about five she and the rest of the family (two older boys and one older girl) talked with me about whether I would like to be adopted, and what that would mean. For me it was an easy choice. I had very little memory of any other family, apart from my sister, and I guessed I could carry on seeing her if I wanted to; but she was a bit odd, didn't really fit in.

Sajela - Growing Up

It was strange to be treated like a child; I think adulthood had come to me very early and it was difficult to suddenly have time for recreation and play. I did not really know what to do with it. When my Uncle went back to the Congo, I was moved out of the centre to live with a family. They were very kind to me, but I never felt like one of them. They never asked me about what had happened to me, and I never told. I tried to blend in. I went to the local school and surprisingly did quite well. I had a lot of help with my English, and my writing, but I managed to pass some GCSE's. I continued to see my brother, but I found it very upsetting as he did not seem to have any memories of a time before we had come to the UK. This made me feel very lonely. No-one was left who shared my past. I was also afraid of most men. I dreamt often of my mother. I would wake up in the night screaming and sweating, imagining myself shut away while my mother was raped over and over again. I tried to block these images out. Sometimes I was successful.

When I finished school Social Services helped me to find a flat where I could go to college and support myself. For the first time ever I felt I had a home. Orthie came to see me sometimes, I tried to tell him stories of the Congo, but he never wanted to hear me, he only wanted to be British, to fit in with his friends. I think he was afraid of what might happen to his lovely life. I struggled on with no final decision as to whether I would be granted asylum. The lawyers did their thing, and I just tried to get on with life.

In 2006 I finally was granted asylum (Orthie already had been granted citizenship when he was adopted). Finally I felt free, sad for my wonderful country that had been ravaged by war, but free to go about my life without looking over my shoulder. It was soon after that that Orthie learnt the truth about his birth.

Orthie - Learning about my heritage

In 2011 I was 15 years old and at school – hoping to go off to university after my A levels. There was a gig on at the youth festival, so arriving early I settled myself into the corner of the bar area wait for Gina my girlfriend. There was a young woman talking loudly on the next table. She caught my attention because she was talking about the Democratic Republic of Congo, the war and the "brutal rape of the women of the land". I remember those words especially, and I leaned closer drinking in her words. I remember feeling cold all over, and sweating at the same time, which seemed curious. When the band started up I got up and left.

I rang Sajela. I had not had much contact with her in the last few years, but she was the one person who could give me some information. The missing piece so to speak.

Sajela talked to me about my country. About our mother. She sobbed as she told me about the rape of the women of the village, about my mother. How she died after giving birth to me, the son of one of one of her rapists. I felt nauseous, I was sick, vomiting over the carpet. I felt so much shame for being alive, for not knowing any of this, or even caring enough to ask. How could I rid myself from such atrocities when they were part of my blood? How could I make sense of it?

Sajela took me back home and told my mum what had happened. It was late so she stayed the night, the first time she had ever done that and whilst she was sleeping I went onto the internet and accessed every article I could find about The Democratic Republic of Congo and the war. What I learnt burnt images onto my brain, images that no person should have; images that were not just about people in a far of country; but about me, about my mother, my father, my uncle, my sister. They were images of Armageddon; of genocide, of torture.

I learnt that in the Democratic Republic of Congo it is estimated that 5,000,000 people have died since the beginning of the war. I read an article with accounts of women (and girls as young as 3) who have been raped and tortured. In one of the articles Anneka Van Woudenberg, who is the senior Congo researcher at Human Rights Watch was interviewed and said, "I think because of the widespread nature of the war, because there has been so much violence, rape is now on a daily basis-rape is the norm" her interviewer asks, "women get raped in wars all the time. How is it different here?" She replies, "I think what's different in Congo is the scale and the systematic nature of it, indeed, as well, the brutality. This is not rape because soldiers have got bored and have nothing to do. It is a way to ensure that communities accept the power and authority of that particular armed group. This is about showing terror. This is about using it as a weapon of war," she explains.[2]

It is a vast country over 900,000 square miles (almost as big as the USA). It is a country rich in mineral wealth with copper, cobalt, diamonds, gold, tantalum, petroleum and other minerals. Crops such as coffee, tea, rubber, cocoa and palm oil can be grown in the fertile soil. This should be a wonderful country, a country that is able to support **all** of its people without **anyone** starving to death.

Sajela – talking about the past

I suppose all my life, since Orthie was adopted, I waited for him to ask me about his mother, about our life in the Congo. In the early days it would have been easy for me to talk to him, as time passed, and he grew up English, it became something that may not happen. I got on with my life, trained as a nurse and got a job in a general medical ward of the local hospital. When he did finally ask, it shocked me to the core of my being. I had never thought about him being the son of one of my mother's rapists. To me, he was always my mother's son; my little brother. I never really gave thought to the circumstances of his conception. To him though, it seemed as if this was the only thing of importance. He was the son of terrorists. He did not want this heritage. I was frightened for his life. He seemed to reject everything, including me. "Why did you not kill me at birth?" he asked. "It would have been better if you had killed me at birth, than allow a monster to be born". I stayed with him the night and he spent the night surfing the net. Looking at articles about the war; despairing.

In the morning I left to go back to work. We promised to meet again the following evening, but he cancelled. He kept cancelling, and I had my own problems; I had just discovered I was pregnant. When I next saw Orthie some months later he had changed beyond recognition. He had stopped washing, looked uncared for, told me he had dropped out of school. His adoptive mum told me that she thought he was taking drugs, staying out late and the school authorities had given up on him. She was really worried; I realised in that moment that she really loved him. She was now his mother, and that was ok.

---

[2] For more details of this interview see:
http://www.cbsnews.com/2100-18560_162-3701249.html

Orthie – repercussions

After the day of revelations it was hard to get back into my old life. I had become someone else. I lost my way. I found different friends. I wanted to do reckless things. We tried to run across the rooftops of local buildings one night and were arrested. I spent much time drinking and I started taking all manner of drugs; anything to stop me thinking, or being. I failed all my exams, well I did not even go to most of them! Then followed a life of crime; partly to feed the habit, but mostly because I didn't care what I did. I dropped out of school. We broke into houses of friends, stole cars, gear from other druggies. I even stole from my sister when she visited. Violence became what we did best. Warfare erupted between the Asian and Black gangs. Pub windows were smashed, a warehouse was set on fire. Young women were defiled. "What did it matter?" I thought. My father after all was a terrorist, a rapist. The violence gave vent to my anger.

I guess it would have gone on longer if I hadn't overdosed; I could easily have ended up in prison. However, I ended up in hospital with needles sticking out my arm, my sister and adoptive mum at my bedside. I think I had some kind of breakdown. I cannot remember much about the months that followed. I went to some rehabilitation mental health centre. They got me, somehow, living again. I didn't want to live, but I didn't have the energy to fight both of them and the system.

Leaving the centre was a huge thing. My mum and sister were brilliant, they were my rocks. I clung to my sister especially; she was the only one who could help me make any sense of this shit that I called my life.

Sajela – ways forward

After Orthie had his breakdown we decided that it was time to try to make sense of our lives. By this time I was working for a small project offering support to asylum seekers, providing basic health information and services. I also had a baby daughter and was struggling with trying to juggle work with being a single mum. Orthie's mum was really supportive, also he attended the local drug and alcohol project and was able to access some counselling. After a while we both started to go to see a therapist together, but it was hard for Orthie to talk about his feelings without him falling back into taking drugs or alcohol, and hard for me to witness his despair. I think my feelings mainly were that of anger. Anger at a world which allowed refugees (who I saw every day at work) be traumatised by the place they had come to seek sanctuary. People often came into the centre at work with no money to live, no where to stay, and no hope for the future. Anger also at a world that ignored the conflict in the Congo, just shut its eyes to the genocide and rape of a country in the name of… What?

I'm not sure those engaged in the violence even know. I feel sad for my country, for my daughter, who will never know the beauty of that land far away.

Orthie - story telling

Talking to someone about my feelings was really hard. I was afraid of disintegrating, of the feelings overwhelming me, of going back to drugs. The call of them is always there, it lurks in the mind like an unwanted skin.

Our counsellor suggested that perhaps writing our story may be helpful, and she showed us some stories written by a colleague of hers who was writing with people about trauma. We started to keep journals, and show them to each other and our counsellor. I contacted her colleague (Sue) who was very interested in our accounts.

Working with our counsellor, and Sue, has been great. Trying to make a coherent story out of all the bits has been really helpful, and having it published means that our lives are worth something, and will perhaps draw attention of other people to what is happening in the world around us. My next step, I feel is to one day visit my homeland. I want to somehow make some difference into what is happening there. I cannot, I realise, alter my genes, but I can strive to fight against the war and the rape of people. I can start to join with others who, thanks to the UK, have an education and can make a difference. I have enrolled in college on a journalism and media course, and do some voluntary work for an African charity, I am honing my skills, I feel, to one day write the next instalment in my life; a different ending to a story of tragedy. I look at my niece, and her happiness with life, and it seems a distinct possibility. My mum and Sajela have really encouraged me, they have seen hope even when I cannot see it.

Part IV

Breaking the Bonds of Secrecy

CHAPTER ELEVEN

INTEGRATING NARRATIVES WITH THEORY

Although this book and small qualitative study does not aim to be a learned thesis on the theories of trauma, I felt that at this point it may be pertinent to tease out what is meant by the terms intergenerational, and transgenerational trauma, and what has been learned about these concepts from the stories of the contributors.

Firstly, by "intergenerational" trauma, I mean trauma passed down directly from one generation to another. For example Joy's experience of living with her mother who had been traumatised by childhood sexual abuse directly affected her. By "transgenerational" I mean trauma transmitted across a number of generations, for example Matthew comments, "my mother was affected by domestic violence, as was her mother before her". This transgenerational effect is often also evident in countries at war. This kind of trauma it seems becomes embedded in not just the generations of one family, but throughout the society and culture in which communities live. It becomes a cultural trauma spreading across generations. As Sajela points out, "in the Democratic Republic of Congo it seems as if all generations; all people are affected by the violence. My grandfather, for example, was killed in the Shala war in the late 1970's".

Before turning to the experiences of the contributors however, it seems important to also consider what the literature and research surrounding transmission of trauma, both in the context of war, and also in the context of childhood abuse tell us.

Transmission of trauma in War

Conflict and violence between people has been with us since the beginning of recorded time, and probably pre-dates all records. Nations have constantly invaded, and defended, nations. Different factions of people within nations have vied for power and control using coercion and violence to enforce their authority. There is a traumatic impact from war both for those on the front lines facing the enemy, and also for those not involved with the fighting but caught in the middle. For both there is often horrific injury, loss of loved ones, places and things of value; and a crossing of long held moral codes of behaviour. What is acceptable behaviour in war time is not necessarily acceptable within everyday life; for example murder; the deliberate killing of others. The traumatic memories of war infiltrate the present. Sassoon, quoted by Fussell writes of the First World War,

> "Shell shock. How many a brief bombardment had its long delayed after-effect in the minds of these survivors. Not then was their evil hour, but now; now in the sweating suffocation of nightmare, in paralysis of limbs, in the stammering of dislocated speech. In the name of civilisation these soldiers had been martyred, and it remained for civilisation to prove that their martyrdom wasn't a dirty swindle" (Fussell 1983:141).

What happens to people living in societies where war; and the violence that comes with that are rife? Well there has been much research into the psychological effects of the two world wars (Kardiner and Spiegel 1947; Rosenheck 1986; Helzer et al. 1987; Meares 2000), and in particular the effects of the holocaust where millions of Jews were exterminated (Schab 2010). Research has also extended to both the effects of war on the following generations (Virag 1984; Reichel 1989), and society as a whole (Bracken, Giller, and Summerfield 1995). Ordinary people have, after all, been made extraordinary in that they have both delivered violence (outside of their normal moral code) and experienced violence as a result of others actions. Atkinson makes what seems to me a very pertinent point that, "violence is therefore both an activity and an experience" (Atkinson 2002:11). She goes on to say:

> "The word experience is used to acknowledge that a person (including a child) who is violated in an act of violence experiences violence; that a person who commits violence experiences violence, and that a person who sees or hears violence experience violence. 'Experience' is used as both a verb and a noun'"(ibid:11).

There is also the experience of living, long term, in a war zone, and the societal effects and changes that happen. In the Second World War for example, people who lived through those times often note a sense of "community spirit", of objectifying and vilifying "the enemy" and that they, "spent time with people they would not normally socialise with". An interesting study was carried out by Afana et al. (2010) which looked at the social representations of trauma and the way it is defined by Palestinians living in the Gaza strip. The authors found that these could be classified into three main groups: trauma as a sudden blow with immediate impact, secondly, tragedy; usually to describe an extraordinary event, for example, the loss of a loved one and thirdly traumatic events which are persistent and have long lasting consequences. As the author's write, "the devastating consequences of political violence involve multiple psychological, social, economic, and environmental challenges to the integrity of an individual and to communal life" (Afana et al. 2010:83). There is trauma for societies torn by war on many levels. Sajela and Orthie's stories come from the context of these multiple traumas. As Stearns points out, the conflict within the Democratic Republic of Congo is complex. There is no one common enemy who can be vilified and united against. One of the contributors to his book comments: "You know, you can't really explain these things. For us soldiers, killing comes easy. It has become part of our lives. I have lost five members of my family during the war. You have to understand that"(Stearns 2011:10). The fabric of society and how people identify themselves becomes fragmented; conflict interfering with individual sense of identity (Das 2007).

Within this fragmentation, and different social structure, transmission of trauma across many generations seems possible. Sajela tells me:

> "The cycles of violence experienced by generations of people; which included my grandparents, my mother, and then me; what we did not have was a sense of community and being together without atrocity. Within the society we lived there became no order. Even in the city; Kinshasa was a huge city with all the trappings of a western one. There were offices, and suited men working (although they were rarely paid). People still didn't have running water or consistent electricity though!
>
> Although there was so much fear and trauma and fear in what was happening, the way our society was, was devoid of emotion. It was always about survival, how we were going to survive, not how were we going to cope emotionally. I think it was the same for the people who carried out these atrocities. We had somehow all become sub-human, not connected to each other in any ways. Our sense of who we were; and who others were, was constantly shattered."

Orthie tells me,

> "Although I did not grow up in a war zone; in fact my early childhood was marked by a real sense of belonging to a community, and I resisted very strongly any attempt to wrest that sense of community from me! When I was suddenly aware of the circumstances of my birth, and the wars, I was catapulted into the conflict. Everything was fractured and broken, every

sense of self that I had disappeared in a flash. Nothing made sense at all. There was only Sajela who linked the pieces. I felt totally traumatised, not just by the news of who I was, but by the history that had led to this and the breaking apart of everything I thought was human."

So having looked at a little of the literature regarding transmission of trauma across generations in War, and heard from Sajela and Orthie caught up in war; it is time to explore whether there are any similarities or differences for the families of people affected by childhood abuse and violence?

Transmission of Trauma in Families Affected by Childhood Abuse or Violence

There is now a growing body of literature showing that parents who have been sexually abused as children, especially if they show symptoms of PTSD, pass on some of these traumatic symptoms to their children (Putman 2003). Yehuda, Halligan and Grossman (2001) found evidence of changes to cortisol[1] levels in children with parents who had been affected by childhood abuse, these were similar to those of the children of veterans of armed conflict. They concluded that, "the experience of childhood trauma may be an important factor in the transmission of PTSD from parent to child" (Yehuda, Halligan, and Grossman 2001:733). McCloskey and Bailey (2000) concluded that a, "maternal sexual abuse history indicates a strong potential for the intergenerational transmission of child sexual abuse" (McCloskey and Bailey 2000:1019).

Evidence has also been found of the trans-generational transmission of trauma across multiple generations where childhood sexual abuse or violence has been reported (Yehuda et al. 2005; Rodriguez et al. 1997).

The literature relating to children witnessing domestic violence, or living with a parent who was physically abused as a child seem to convey a similar message. A comprehensive twenty year study of 543 children growing into adults confirms the trend towards behaviour patterns consistent with the transmission of trauma, e.g. conduct disorders, substance misuse, mental health issues (Ehrensaft, Cohen, Brown,

---

[1] Cortisol is a hormone secreted by the adrenal glands. It is secreted in higher levels during the "fight of flight" response to stress. for more information see: http://stress.about.com/od/stresshealth/a/cortisol.htm

Smailes, Chen, and Johnson 2003). What do these statistics mean? Are they relevant?

> *Journal 25th July 2012*
>
> *I am trying to write about inter and transgenerational aspects of childhood sexual abuse and violence, and although I can picture in my mind what needs to be said the words remain illusive. They seem like grains of sand that slip through my hand without sticking together.*
>
> *The contributors all comment that it is easy to talk about their experiences, in terms of thoughts, feelings and behaviours, but it is really difficult to analyse what has happened in their (and my) relationships through the generations. Also there is literature and research which I am reading, which somehow do not feel resonant with the experiences. Words seem missing, and there are gaps which are very hard to fill.*
>
> *I turn back to reading the words of others, Schwab explores her experiences of growing up German in a post war Germany, "traumatic silences and gaps in language are, if not mutilations and distortions of the signifying process, ambivalent attempts to conceal. But indirectly, they express trauma otherwise shrouded in secrecy or relegated to the unconscious". (Schwab 2010:4).*
>
> *There is something about the secrets and gaps of processing emotion from the past which seep into the present, and make it very difficult to fill, especially to write about.*

Etherington states, "childhood trauma creates chaos in many people's lives and chaos can leave us speechless, voiceless and silenced" (Etherington 2003:9), and certainly that sense of being voiceless is one that I experience trying to write about the effects of childhood trauma. I talk about this with Joy who has spoken in earlier chapters about things that are difficult to speak about, and how this leads to ice forming between people. She emails me:

> Hi Sue,
>
> Yes, I think there is a real problem here. Partly I think because the story line belongs to someone else, so you (or should I say I) can have the feelings, and the behaviour patters; the trauma basically, but you never have all the facts. So you can never process what has gone on in the past. You can make some sense of the bits you know about, but there is so much that is never known about. For example: I learnt a lot about my mother and what happened to her, but there were some things I never knew; when it

started? The words he used to ensure her silence? When it stopped? The story was completely fragmented. This makes it very difficult to process. When we have problems of our own in the past; we can take the memories out of the cupboard in our mind and go through them; and then put them away, in order, so to speak. When the problems are someone else's however; there is nothing we can do; especially if that person becomes unwell, and unable to say anything.

It is a bit like being Miss Marple! trying to find clues that make sense of it all and bridge the gaps. There is this whole culture, going back at least a generation, to my grandparents at least, and going forward into the next one … if I am not careful; of silence and a real fragmenting of normal family relationships.

Hi Joy,

I am really interested in what you are saying here. I agree this has to do with a culture of silence, a culture that if we are not careful gets passed on, and also speaks to me about your mother not being able to process what had happened to her, in the same way that memories are normally processed, because what happened to her was just so traumatic. What got passed on to you was not really the history of something that had happened, but unprocessed feelings and behaviours.

Does this make any sense?

Hi Sue,

Yes. Absolutely; when I have talked to my mother, I often get her feelings, and some of the shocking detail, but it is never in a coherent history or story. I can never piece together what happened and therefore relegate it to the past. It appears to haunt her, and to an extent me, in the here and now.

It is like constructing this random jigsaw puzzle that has a huge plate of spaghetti on it. Nothing really seems to make sense. I did find some of the pieces (perhaps the edges!) when I talked to my great aunt at a recent family wedding. My great grandmother apparently came from a very good, well to do background, but was disowned when she became pregnant with my grandmother. It is not known who the father was, but there were suspicions that to quote my great aunt, "things weren't as they should have been in the family after her father came back from the war". I guessed she meant the First World War.

All the time there is this real silence around what was happening. People not talking to each other in the same family; that silence that I have talked about being between people.

Something else clicked into place when I was reading the stories from Sajela I really got this feeling of a whole society that had somehow got into patterns of behaving where there were gaps between what was happening, and what people wanted of their lives. Violence had become accepted as "normal". Even though to me as an outsider it seemed anything but normal. I guess where I saw the similarity was that in some ways within my family, this silence, the abuse, was somehow accepted as normal, or not spoken about. No-one liked or approved of it, but no-one was jumping up and down and saying, "this should not be happening", or even "this should never have happened" and it repeated down the line. My great grandmother, whatever happened to her, it does not sound happy or healthy, or talked about … my grandfather abusing my mother, my mother telling me about the abuse, which in a strange way also felt abusive. The words used were emotive, but the emotion regarding what had happened was absent.

I am determined to stop this kind abuse with me. My daughter should not have to have this kind of legacy passed on to her, yet if I tell her nothing; is that just prolonging the secrecy?

I was interested that Joy talked of legacies. Schwab also speaks of the inter and transgenerational transmission of trauma as haunting legacies (Schwab 2010). She writes:

> "The transmission of violent legacies by far exceeds the passing on of historical knowledge or even of stories with thick descriptions of personal involvement. What I call 'haunting legacies' are things hard to recount or even to remember, the results of a violence that holds an unrelenting grip on the memory yet is deemed unspeakable" (Schwab 2010:1).

Patrick emails

Hi Sue,

This kind of passing the trauma on to the next generation, or generations, I guess in some cases seems really important for us to understand. I have been reading a book called the Shell and the Kernal by Abraham and Torok, they talk about the haunting quality of the traumatic memories of others. I really resonated with this. As you know having flashbacks from something that happened to my father really made me doubt my sanity. He says something like: It is the buried tombs of other people's ghosts that come back to haunt the children or descendents, and it is those descendents who have to lay them to rest (Abraham and Torok 1994). How can we lay them to rest though?

It seems from what I have read, that to lay them to rest would involve telling the stories of the events and somehow processing the memories. How can this be done however when they are not my memories to process?

Dear Patrick,

I think you are right, and I am not sure that I have an answer to your questions. I wonder whether you may be interested in meeting with other contributors who have similar, yet different, experiences to talk about this?

Dear Sue,

Yes. Yes of course. That would be really helpful I think. Just talking about these things in the open really makes a difference. They feel different. Transparent. Not secret any more.

Journal September 2012

There is also something prevalent within this work around whether contributors are, or feel, free to speak about stories that relate to others. It is more than just thinking about confidentiality, and not breaking the confidentiality of others who have not given their permission. I feel it within my very bones. A real reluctance to talk about my mother's experiences, as if the silence once broken would break apart the fabric of everything, my family, my life and the lives of others.. "How much of this story is mine to tell?" muses Patrick. A comment I resonate with.

Abarbanel makes the point in narrating her own life and therapeutic journey in the wake of childhood abuse, "I believe that my ability to heal from my trauma depended on realising that I had a right to my narrative" (Abarbanel 2012:17). I read her words and intellectually I can understand what she is saying, but there is still a strong reluctance within me to break the silence imposed by my mother, who died some years ago, and her siblings, still alive. I recognise however that this silence and the inability of the family to talk about things caused great anguish to my late brother and his family. Is there any way or ways round this I wonder? Can we (myself, and the contributors) find ways to break the silence and move forward from being trapped in a trauma that does not belong to us. How can we lay these memories down to rest?

Etherington, referring to Whitfield (1995) makes a very helpful point that,

> "in transforming trauma we need to recognise the role of memory. Memory is not necessarily a factual, coherent or linear record of something that actually happened. Rather it is a process of bringing together parts of our experience to create a coherent and organised whole" (Etherington 2003:32).

She goes on to speak of how transformation of trauma does not depend on coherent memories but rather a, "'gathering together' of different kinds of information, images metaphors and responses" (ibid:32). We need, she feels, "new stories about our lives and new meanings" (ibid:32).

If we are indeed to create new meanings and stories from what feels at the moment fragments of memory and affect. How could we do this I wonder?

CHAPTER TWELVE

PEACE AND JUSTICE

Having met with, and listened to the contributors in this book (and many other people over my years as psychotherapist who have influenced my thinking greatly) it felt important to find a way of using this writing and research to challenge the predominating stories of abuse and violence which were being passed through the generations, because these excluded other stories people could tell of their lives, that were more liberating; and hope filled. Whilst the events which had so traumatised families were seen as "defining" of the person, or family, they remained trapped as, "victims" or "survivors", of these events. One way I have used in the past to enable people to re-author, or redefine, the stories they tell of their lives comes from the work of anthropologist Barbara Myerhoff (1979; 1986; 1982), and was developed for therapeutic practice by narrative therapists such as the late Michael White, and David Epston (White 2000; White and Epston 1990). It is usually referred to as "definitional ceremony" or "outsider witness practices". I have written a little in chapter seven, and more fully about the theoretical concepts of these practices elsewhere (Dale 2010, 2011), here I wanted to give the reader a flavour of what happens at a definitional ceremony and something of the process in action.

We met together in my small consulting room in mid-Wales. Orthie was to be at the centre of the process, his sister Sajela, three other research contributors: Duncan Joy and Patrick, Orthie's counsellor and one of my counselling supervisees were to act as witnesses; I was to act as interviewer. We decided to video record and sound record our meeting and that the video recording would be retained by Orthie to remind him of the events which had taken place, and the sound recording would be retained by me and could be used for the purpose of writing this book.

Prior to the ceremony I had provided everyone with guidelines for definitional ceremonies based on those written by Michael White (2003). I had also talked with Orthie, his mum and witnesses at length to ensure they were confident and sure about taking part in such a ceremony.

It was a long journey for most. Mid Wales is very beautiful, but apart from myself, and my supervisee, everyone was travelling for over two hours. We started therefore with coffee and sandwiches over which we talked informally making introductions, looking again at the guidelines for definitional ceremonies, which had previously been distributed, and ensuring we were all happy with the agreed ground rules regarding confidentiality and recording. We also tested out both the visual and audio recording devices.

When we were ready, we started. What follows is an edited transcript of some of the initial questions and responses by Orthie, followed by the edited responses of some of the witnesses. We have chosen to edit some of the conversation as following the ceremony there was a general consensus that whilst all of the words spoken were helpful, some of them needed to remain confidential as they involved third parties who could not give permissions. This editing has largely been done by me, but agreed by us all.

Orthie and I were sat where Orthie could see me, but where he was apart and positioned such that he did not have to give eye contact to the others, who were sitting in the position of an audience. My sight is such that whilst looking at Orthie I could not see anyone else.

Definitional Ceremony in Action

Sue: I know from earlier conversations that there are many stories you could tell of your life. Have you had any thoughts about what you would like to talk about today? What would make a difference?

Orthie: Yes. I have thought about it a lot, and yes, there are many things I could speak about that feel important… The Congo.. What is happening in that country and how that affects me, my relationship with my family, the whole story of seeking asylum.. I think though, what is in my mind, and perhaps up 'til now I haven't really allowed myself to think about is what happened to my mother, and how learning about that tipped me off the edge..

Sue: tipped you off the edge…. does this feel a safe enough place to talk about that?

Orthie: Yes… Yes.. I want to talk about it. I am not going there again! (laughs)

Sue: I am so glad to hear that! I am wondering what this, "tipping of the edge" was like for you? Is that something you would like to speak about, or would you prefer to talk about your mother?

Orthie: Tipping off the edge was like spiralling out of control, without a parachute, from a jet. The jet carries on flying, and you are just left there tumbling through space. Terrified. Eventually you try to adopt some kind of pose that helps you fly through the air with the least resistance.

I think that when I realised that my mother's rape had resulted in my conception it just flipped something in my brain. I was not the person I wanted, or hoped, to be. I was the son of rapists, unnamed. Everything I was sure about in life was suddenly put into question. It felt that I, myself, had been raped, the trauma of that was enormous. I think that is why I started drinking, and ultimately what led to the heroin. Heroin is a cruel mistress, she beckons seductively, then ties you up so that you can never escape, apart from through dying…….

Sue: I wonder… you say dying. Did dying seem like an option?

Orthie: Yes of course. Often. I often wished that I was dead, even had a sort of plan for that to happen.

Sue: Yet you chose to live? You are still here.. There must have been something about life that you held onto?

Orthie: Wishing you are dead, and actually doing the dying, are two very different things. Wishing you were dead is like a fantasy about having some control over life that has got beyond all other controls, actually doing it takes energy and commitment, and I don't think that I had either of those. There was also this little thread, this glimmer of silvery hope. Hope that it would get better. I sense it here today; a hope that my, and other people's words, will make a small change; even if it is to just one or two people.

Sue: I am wondering whether you want to talk a little more about that glimmer of silvery hope, or what that small change might look like?

Orthie: The hope is about feeling listened to. About being heard by others, and them accepting me for all that I am. It is about other people noticing that atrocities are happening in my birth country that are affecting real people, just like them. It is about accepting myself. That even with the genes I have. I am ok.

Sue: That last one seems like a biggie……

Orthie: Yes, I think that it is probably the biggest of all. It is huge. Even saying the words out loud. There is shame in my heart. Shame that even wanting to accept myself is a colluding with what happened…..

Sue: Shame tells you that accepting yourself is colluding with what happened…. that sounds really difficult? I am wondering if you have any choices here?

Orthie: I think that perhaps, "shame" is a bit like heroin. It is a cruel mistress who beats me, if I let it! I suppose one of my choices is to ditch her! What I mean is that perhaps I have to let go of her. I am, after all, who I am. I cannot change my genetic make up, even as I cannot change the colour of my skin. I can however live my life without the ghost of my father (who I have never known) standing on my shoulder. I can choose to live my life respecting women and fighting for justice for my countrymen and women.

Sue: When you say, "I can choose to live my life respecting women and fighting for justice for my countrymen and women" I feel your passion, and for me it brings tears near to the surface…

(Orthie weeps silently)

Orthie: Yes. Tears wash away so much. There are so many tears that I have never dared shed.

Sue: You have been afraid of the tears?

Orthie: Yes. They mean acceptance. Acceptance that this happened, that I have to live with it. That there is no escape.

Sue: Is it ok for the tears to be here with us today? Or would you like us to stop or take a break?

Orthie: I think it is very ok for the tears to be with us today. They are such a relief, and to share them here is fine. Your tears help also, they tell me you are standing with me – I could always find **you** a tissue! (laughter)

Our conversation carries on for another twenty minutes where Orthie outlines the story of their families flight from the Democratic Republic of the Congo and what happened to them as they sought asylum.

After a short break we re-group. This time with myself and the witnesses taking centre stage. I ask the group if any of them have heard within Orthie's story anything that has resonated with themes from their own life stories.

Patrick starts off the proceedings by telling the story of his own experiences of learning about his father's abuse and then goes on to talk about the words Orthie used which resonated for him. These were about Orthie's descriptions of shame.

> Patrick: When I learnt what had happened to my father at the hands of a priest, and I had chosen to become a priest, I felt that the shame would completely destroy me. When Orthie talked about shame as similar to heroin, and a, "hard mistress", I realised that, yes, it really intruded almost like a kind of extension of the abuser. As Orthie was speaking I realised that I did not want to carry anything of him, the abuser, around with me. He was not worth my time. My father had carried him around for a very long time, and still does, and this is a very heavy burden. I realised that I could choose not to do this, and this brought tears to my eyes.
>
> Sue: Do you want to talk any more about these tears?
>
> Patrick: Yes. And, no. I suppose as a man, I have always shied away from them. But somehow your, and Orthie's, tears gave me permission to allow them to fall. I realise, probably a bit late in life (laughs) that it is ok to "feel", that I will not melt from a few tears! Sharing them together felt like an act of unity.

Joy then tells the story of her finding out that her grandfather was also her natural father and how this also resulted in her feeling that she was also, "tipping of the edge".

> Joy: "Tipping off the edge" was the phrase that stood out for me. I could feel it in my body as Orthie spoke. It felt like vertigo. The feeling I had when I realised who my natural father was. Everything that I had thought and known to be true suddenly slipped away and yes I was left with shame.
>
> Sue: Were there any images that came to mind that changed this "slipping away"?
>
> Joy: Yes. The, "silvery glimmer of hope" I saw it in my minds eye. A small shimmering thread amongst a tapestry of dark strident colours. The hope of something different.
>
> I also toyed with the idea of killing myself. I am not quite sure why I didn't, except that the other people in my life; my daughter, the people I

> really cared about were more important than what I wanted. I clung to this I think.
>
> It is strange, although others have spoken of "tears". For me, I have shed so many tears, that today was about feeling joy. The joy of hope for something different, for a life where I do not have to carry my grandfather with me. For me it is a relief. A letting go.
>
> Sue: are there any images for you about what that letting go might be like?
>
> Joy: I think that it is like a nutshell travelling along a small stream allowing the water to propel it. Not fighting or resisting, just going with the flow and allowing yourself to be poured over a waterfall, the weightlessness of the fall, then the beauty of finding yourself in a slow moving beautiful river full of clean bright water.

Joy goes on to talk about her hopes and dreams for the future, and about her relationship with her daughter. Duncan then joins the conversation. He picks up on the theme that Orthie had outlined of wishing he was dead:

> Duncan: I think the thing Orthie said which really resonated with my own life was when he talked about wanting to be dead, but not having the energy to do anything about it.
>
> Sue: Can you remember the phrase he used which resonated?
>
> Duncan: I think it was something like, "a fantasy about having some control over life that has got beyond all other controls", and it was something about this concept of fantasy which gave control which suddenly made me sit up and think, "yes, I do that too".
>
> Sue: Can you say a bit more about how you do this too?
>
> Duncan: Yes. I think I have told you Sue, about how I used to fantasise about being a girl instead of a boy, and this helped me get through trying to make sense of the violence exhibited by my step-fathers towards my mother. Somehow the fantasy of being someone else, or even having part of me that was someone else, who was not violent or aggressive, was a life saver. When it came to it though I couldn't hold on to that way of coping. I found myself to be heterosexual and despite my best efforts, I too became angry and aggressive when my partner crossed an invisible thread of behaviour which I found tolerable. Not having this fantasy I also slipped into the abyss.
>
> Sue: I wonder how you managed to find your way out of this abyss?

> Duncan: I think I fell for a long time and then became suspended in some kind of web of depression. Talking with my brother was probably the starting point for me. Sharing our feelings, making contact with another person, real contact. Crying together. That is the start. Crying here also helps me. It feels that perhaps these tears are in fact the silvery threads that Orthie refers to? For me anyway they have felt life saving.

Other stories were told that will be recounted on another occasion perhaps, the themes reiterated those given about the metaphors used by Orthie describing, "tipping off the edge"; "feelings of wanting to die" the "silvery thread of hope" and the liberating properties of tears. Following these witnesses re-telling of the stories we had a short break. When we re-convened I re-interviewed Orthie.

> Sue: In light of what you have heard this morning, has anything changed for you?
>
> Orthie: So much. I am not really sure how to speak of it. I think it feels a bit like coming home. Finding a real sense of community, and family. An affirmation that I am not going, and have never been mad, or bad! It feels like being lifted up.
>
> Sue: Could you say a bit more about this "lifted up".
>
> Orthie: I think the lifted up is being supported by a criss-cross of silver threads. Threads coming from the hope (and tears) I have heard in other people. I feel connected finally to a other people. I have hope that other people will listen, and care about, what we have said and that their threads of hope will join ours. This feels really good, and possible to move forward from. In my mind I see a giant trampoline where I can bounce and soar over the hurdles that come in front of me.
>
> I have loved also hearing Sajela talking more about her experiences. I think in the past I have always avoided my connection to her, because I have felt so much shame and guilt. Now though I feel I can look at her and realise I have a sister. Of my blood. Together we can help others who are trying to fight for justice in their countries. Even in this country there are so many injustices. Perhaps I have the hope that others will speak out.

Our conversations went on for some time, and were filled with hope and plans. I hope that this small excerpt has given the reader some understanding of the process of a definitional ceremony in action. It was a dynamic process where all of us were left changed. We moved from being separate people with stories of pain and despair to a vibrant community with hope for a future and defined not by abusive acts, but by so many hopeful stories of our lives. The connections between us were strong.

CHAPTER THIRTEEN

A COLLECTIVE BIOGRAPHY EXPLORING INTERGENERATIONAL TRAUMA

Following on from the definitional ceremony we wanted to find a way of capturing some of our new understandings about ourselves and our movement away from the effects of trauma, and also work as a group to produce some writing that may shed some light on intergenerational trauma. I suggested that we think about using a "collective biography" writing style, and turned to a narrative research model developed for social science researchers.

Firstly, I think before I define what I mean by, "collective biography" it would be helpful to consider how this methodology was developed. It originally came from the work of social science researchers, Bronwyn Davies and Susanne Gannon (2006), out of an original feminist and social constructionist research methodology described as, "memory work" (Haug 1987) that was introduced by Haug and her colleagues explicitly to, "bridge the gap between theory and experience" (Onyx and Small 2001:773), and to address the perceived gap between these women's experience and Marxist theory which dominated the political landscape of their lives (Davies and Gannon 2006). This was a group method, which involved the researchers collectively analysing their written memories.

Davies and Gannon drawing on this strategy but moving away from what was perceived as Haug's, "quarrel with Marxism" (Davies and Gannon 2006:4) wanted to examine the thoughts and practices which were normally taken for granted, and thought to be not in need of re-examination.

Davises and Gannon and their participants, all women, gathered over a series of days specifically to look within their own memories (usually connected with themes of gender and power) and to write; producing, "an embodied sense of what happened" (Davies and Gannon 2006:3) within a collective telling. It was hoped to make visible the discourses through which people made meanings and identities; removing through questioning of the stories, the vague and unclear, stripping away the taken for granted clichés we often use to describe life. This process was not intended to be the, "warm fuzzy pursuit of empathy" (Davies 2000:19) but a questioning and challenging of individual stories such that the writing produced sought, "to avoid the repetition of well-practiced ways of knowing and includes, instead, embodied memories" (Davies et al. 2004:372).

Embodied, as it is used here, I take to mean a moving away from cognitive process and taken for granted theories as to why we might feel as we do; towards reliance on memories drawn into the fabric of our bodies these, "being retrieved in sensations, motor responses, affects, ego states, and images" (Milchman 2003:325). Gannon explains these kinds of memories within her writing:

> "*I don't understand 'embodiment',* she worries
> Until the taste of nectar on her tongue
> Blue bubblegum on pink flesh
> Warm hot piss streaming through clenched thighs
> Sour damp sheets" (Davies and Gannon 2006:118).

The outcomes of these collective studies were not considered to be a universal truth, nor as a means of generating knowledge about the individual self of each person present, nor therapeutic (although sometimes this was a hoped for side-effect) but as a, "means to provide knowledge about the ways in which individuals are made social, are discursively constituted in particular fleshy moments" (Davies and Gannon 2006:3). The task was seen of one of, "interrupting the taken-for-grantedness of everyday discourses and practices" (Davies and Gannon 2006:7). Through an intense "interrogation" of the stories emerging they looked to gain an understanding of the social, and the way individual subjectivities are created and maintained, through specific kinds of discursive practices.

> "Through the telling of and listening to the spoken and written stories and through the questions and answers, we aim to open up spaces in which our stories become not merely autobiographical, but are the means to make visible the discursive processes in which we each have been collectively caught up" (Davies and Gannon 2006:11).

Following the individual writing and questioning of stories within the group meetings, the participants would then collaborate to produce an analytical text using the written memories forming a single narrative of the collective experience. *Becoming Schoolgirls: the ambivalent project of subjectification* (Davies et al. 2001) is one such study which gives an example of how individual accounts become a collective account and challenge to common assumptions.

This telling, and re-telling stories, in theory, seems on the face of it similar to the process of definitional ceremony where people tell multi-layered stories that are connected through common themes. The purpose however is different. Within definitional ceremony the story telling is normally focussed on enabling the person at the centre of the process to strengthen their ties with others, and feel less isolated; within collective biography however, the focus is not so much on any one person, but on the collective account. Jane Speedy, who was running a workshop on collective biography with a group of doctoral students in 2006 commented regarding her attendance at a workshop conducted by Davies and Gannon, "my experience of the workshop was that it was a 'brutal' process, I wanted to develop something that was different and more about 'witnessing' than 'tearing apart'" (Speedy 2006), and to me, this also seemed vitally important. Essentially I wanted always to remain, a therapist first and a social science researcher second. The therapeutic outcome would always be more important than any research outcomes.

Speedy (2005) used a combination of definitional ceremony and collective biography practices to work with a group of young men both therapeutically, and also to produce a collective paper with the notion of creatin, "transgressive writing practices developed by groups at the margins with an interest in telling 'stories against the grain'" (Speedy 2005:32). It was this kind of combination of practices that I wanted to aim for within my own research.

Foucault (Foucault 1980, 1997) speaks of power as existing in relationship rather than belonging to an individual or as an existing entity. He sees these power relations as always present within human relationships, mobile with the ability of changing, even where there is an imbalance of power there is usually some way (even if extreme) for the person to resist domination. The way in which we position ourselves in conversation (or in the writing of others lives) can enable the other to negotiate the power relations between us. Within collective biography the position of researcher and researched are merged. The data emerging from the researchers own memories and text produced is collaborative, the power dynamic within the collective fluid. The writing you will find therefore within the main text of this chapter is owned by all of us, and neither my own voice as editor, nor any one person's voice predominates. We are a collective.

Our collective process began following the definitional ceremony. As shown in the previous chapter there were definite themes and overlaps within the stories told about our lives, but individual stories remained distinct, and individuality was a key factor. Within the collective biography we speak with one voice.

Following the ceremony we all undertook to write something about our personal understandings of intergenerational trauma, we tried to use words and phrases that evoked strong images, and resonated with the themes that had come through strongly in the ceremony, these being, "tipping off the edge", "feelings of wanting to die", the "silvery thread of hope" and "the liberating properties of tears". Some wrote poetry, others prose, these were collated by be into one document that was then circulated, and gradually, with many, many revisions and amendments finally something emerged that somehow encapsulated for all of us both what it meant for us growing up with a parent who was traumatised and where we are going. The document takes the form of a three act play.

Act 1 Tipping off the Edge

A young woman (Fear) enters stage left she perches on bar stool centred in the stage. A man (Anger) enters (stage right) and paces continually in circles around the stool. Another actor (Despair) covered in red cloth already lays unmoving at centre right of stage.

Fear: The world tips vertiginously,
Where can my feet find known ground?
Where am I?
Who am I?
What is this world I find myself in?
Anguish cracks my teeth and melts my bones.
My body betrays me.

I am sick, but no manner of retching brings up the bile.

Anger *(pacing with purpose)*
Why?
What is the point?
How…
    Can this be happening?
I hate…
    Everything, everyone, especially you, especially me.
I despise..
    Everything, everyone, especially you, especially me.
Where is God in all of this?
    Does he exist?
    Do I care!

Fear: Caught in the trap of other people's secrets;
not my place to tell.
Trapped,
alone,
afraid,

Anger: What good does fear do?
Rage is the only answer;
DESTROYING,
DESPOILING,
REVENGEFUL,
TERRIFYING,
(Anger Moves to push Fear off stool)

Fear: *(gets down and hides the other side of the stool)*
Who is there to be angry with?
Only me,
only she, who loved me in the only way she could?
Others,
The dead ones who are dead?

Not like despair over there *(points to despair still lying unmoving under red cloth)*
So isolated,
So alone.
Afraid of anger obliterating me and everything I hold dear.

Afraid of being engulfed by her.
Despair.

Despair (still covered with red cloth moves silently to centre stage and covers all three of them with cloth)

Act Two – Wanting to Die

(Fear, Anger and Despair (still covered in red cloth) all stand centre stage)

All speak together in unison:

Control.
Out of control

Need a way of bringing this back into control.
Cannot go on like this.
No life at all.
(they shake off the red cloth and leave it lying on the ground)

A plan of action is needed.
Goals set.
A way found of stopping the abuse; with me.
A wave of energy comes with planning;
where to do it?
When to do it?
How to do it?

Anger: Could it be the rope?
Fear: Could it be the pills?
Despair: When will it be just ended?

(*A new actor "But" enters stage right)*
But: What about my family?
What about the pain caused to those who love me.
You should feel guilty
You are not a real person,
A real person would care.

Despair: I knew I didn't have the guts for it!

Anger: Worm of a person that you are.
Fear: Trapped. Isolated. Alone.

Act Three – The silvery thread of hope

(All four actors are standing centre stage with the red cloth pooled in front of them they speak in unison)

All: Stuck-ness,
un-welded by the silvery thread of tears *(actors move apart holding between them a long silver rope)*
Tears that liberate
Wash away the glue that binds;
anger, despair and fear.
There are no "Buts" in tears;
in the tears of many combined.
(But leaves stage left)

Fear: Tears of the past mingle with tears of the present
A homogenous stream of light in a dark place
They join us, and you, and humanity in choices.

Choices about what we can do together to change the world?
What do our experiences bring?
Is there anything good that can come out of this dark place?

Anger: Does trauma have to pass on to the next generation,
and the next,
and the next.
What can we do to STOP it in its' tracks?

All: Together a glimpse of hope
A starburst of a future where trauma does not live
Not dependent on our mother
or father,
or grandparents.
Just together with our tears
We can set sail across the mighty river into a new world;
with hope in our hearts and minds.

CHAPTER FOURTEEN

ENDINGS, CONCLUSIONS AND REFLECTIONS

A Researchers Story

Entering into a narrative research project connected with such an emotive subject, and one that I have personal connections with could have been fraught with both ethical and emotional consequences. It has however proved, for me at least, a very positive experience. Before I turn to the contributors to find out their views, I want to just think about the ethical responsibility of telling stories of other people's lives, and to share something of my own journey as a researcher, and also as someone who has grown up with a legacy of childhood sexual abuse.

Speedy (2007) makes the point that when thinking about ethics, and conducting research into counselling, the ethical guidelines provided by the professional bodies such as the BACP[1] make an assumption that, "it is counsellors and not clients who are researching therapeutic practice and that this research is carried out by individuals, not collectives or communities" (Speedy 2007:51). Within research such as that contained in this book however; whilst I have remained aware, and responsive to the fact, that those contributing, especially those who had known me in a therapeutic setting, could be affected emotionally by their involvement with the project; and may relate to me in my role of psychotherapist or counsellor, I have also tried to challenge the traditional power dynamics of the "researcher" and "researched" by not seeing the contributors as "vulnerable" and participants that need, "adequately protecting" (Bond 2004:12), but as a people with a voice and strengths equal to my own. My role was to provide the safe framework in which we could research and write a narrative inquiry, and to provide editing support. I was the one as Patrick stated, "the person to ask the difficult but curious questions that

[1] British Association for Counselling and Psychotherapy

got me thinking". I held an ethical commitment to, "do no harm" but tried at all times to promote contributors autonomy.

The process of research was as much the contributor's task as it was mine and whilst I took on the task of editing, and commenting on written, and conversational, material, what was chosen to be included or excluded was the individual contributors choice. Occasionally I would make suggestions; especially if I felt that the person's anonymity, or that of another, would be compromised. The stories told are not necessarily what I would have chosen; indeed they far surpass anything I would have thought to ask about. The book is written in my name as all of the contributors, after much debate, decided they would prefer to write anonymously.

Journal July 2012

I learnt to tune into my mothers thoughts and feelings; skills I later discovered were called empathy. The chords that bound us together reverberated with her stories. Often funny happenings; for example her attempts to swing full milk churns over her head, or being chased by a goat. Interspersed with these beautiful stories were secrets to be kept and never divulged, even to my brother. The chords of secrets bound us together and even when I was an adult and far from home.

My mother developed Parkinson's Disease at the age of 58. She became frozen, unable to escape the grip of her memories. The drugs which mobilised her, also mobilised the area of her mind which had been locked shut for many years. She wrote to me of her nightmares. Later she wrote to me letters starting: "Dear Mum.." Finally we had swapped roles; I had become her mother and I was just as unable to keep her safe from harm as her natural mother had been. She was stubborn though, my own children tell me that it is a trait I have inherited! She clung on to life until, at nearly ninety, she surrendered. I sat by her bed holding her hand. It was the only time I have seen her truly at peace. She finally opened her eyes and said, "my daughter; thank you". She waited until I had gone, and she had spoken to the rest of the family, then she died. Her secrets; taken to her grave. My role had finally come to an end.

.The stories from all of the contributors have touched my heart, and helped me understand more of my own story in relation to growing up with a mother who was sexually abused as a child. Although all of our stories were set in different contexts, and relating to different families. The themes of keeping secrets seemed key to all, and sharing this among our collective group has had the effect of putting some of them, at least, to rest.

Contributor's feedback

Having sent the draft manuscript out to the contributor's I began to get some responses:

Email from Joy
Hi Sue,

Wow! What stories. Being involved with this project has been life changing. It has not taken away what happened to my mother, or me, in the past, but somehow it does not seem so important any more. Life suddenly seems full of the, "here and now" rather than all the stuff from the past. My daughter is growing up, and we have a good relationship, and that is great. I think there were two main turning points for me. One was seeing my chapter for the first time. Seeing it all typed out; and funnily, one of the things which struck me most was your comments, the ones from your own journal, alongside. This meant I stopped feeling so lonely. The other really important thing was attending the definitional ceremony and hearing other people speak. Although they all came from very different backgrounds and circumstances, there were so many things we had in common.

Thank you so much for allowing me to be part of all of this, and for the courage to share your stories too. I guess it must be harder when you have to have your name published. I am glad to remain anonymous. I will tell people I want to know about what I have written and that is fine.

Email from Patrick
Hi Sue,

Patrick here! Thank you for sending the draft of the book. I have now read it, and corrected a few spelling errors (sorry I couldn't resist playing the part of editor for a change!).

Reading my chapter was really heart stopping. Even though I have looked at it as we have gone along, and taken out, or put in things. I think it is the nakedness of it that struck me. All the other chapters you have introduced. But this was just me, with a voice to say how it was; and my father – by the way I gave it to him to read too, and he was really moved, he asked if he could see the other chapters so I have passed those on, hope that is ok?

Email from Orthie
Hello Sue,

I am writing this from Tanzania, I am currently out here as a volunteer involved in a twinning village project here. Thank you, the summer is going very well. I will be out here for the next three weeks, then going back home to college in London.

As you know I am hoping that working alongside others in the field I will eventually be skilled enough to go back to the Democratic Republic of Congo and do something of good there. At the moment, I am honing my skills. The people here are amazing, both the other project workers and also the people in the village where we are based. What has really surprised me is that the strength, the community spirit, and for that matter most of the hard physical work comes from the women of the community. They are teaching me a lot about gender inequality; not always in very comfortable ways!

It seems strange to be here reading the chapters of our book, but also makes me realise just how far I have come. I think actually the writing, the talking with others and especially that group writing thing we did where we talked about the really bad things, but also that silvery thread of hope. That has in fact given me hope, and here I am, living my life in all its fullness. That was the text used at the amazing church service we had on Sunday over here. Hundreds of people worshipping together and singing, the singing was just incredible, it made my bones cry out from within me! I think I have found some kind of faith being here which is very different, and very new. I know that I am much younger than the others involved with this, but it's like I've suddenly got an extended family with cousins, aunts and uncles and even a grandparent too.

Watch this space – things are moving forwards!

Email from Jason
Hi Sue,

Thank you so much for sending me the draft book, I have literally sat up all night and read it. It is a real page turner.

Thank you for thinking someone like me could be involved with this. I guess there is still so much shame and guilt I feel, and a sense of not being worthy to have a voice or any connection with others who have been the victims of violence.

I think being involved in this has changed so many things. Reading Matt and Duncan's story was really moving, and in fact I have met up with Matt a couple of times to talk, and that has been so helpful. There is a real sense of solidarity, of standing together and just facing that this is how life is now, and I cannot change the past, but perhaps I can live differently in the future.

Email from Sajela
Hi Sue,

So glad to hear that the work is nearly done! I have benefitted so much from this project – I have my brother back. Thank you!

I have always known that what is happening in the Congo, and our stories were worth writing, but never thought I would have the skill or courage to do it. Doing it this way means that not only is our story out there bringing a little attention to a forgotten part of the world, but also it has been like a course of therapy. We have both moved into a different place. I have moved in my mourning of my mother, and losing Orthie; who I had considered my son, to gaining a brother, and a friend; no, actually, many friends. The depth of feeling that came from the definitional ceremony means I now have a new extended family. For that I am grateful.

I do not think I ever want to go back to the Congo, it has too many difficult memories for me. My life, my family, my work are all here. I think I am finally British!

Email from Elsa:
Dear Sue,

Thank you again for being a "supporter" but also for letting me be one of yours in this book. I am still doing really well. I occasionally have a blip, but these are becoming less, and the good bits are taking over.

I have started going to a local MIND drop in as a volunteer, and that is really great. I have made lots of friends; and I even manage to speak without being spoken to first – quite a miracle I think.

I have read most of the book – well all the stories, the other bits I couldn't concentrate on very well, but I guess that doesn't really matter does it!

Email from Jack
Dear Susan,

You do not know me, but I am the man you call Patrick's father.

I wanted to take the opportunity to thank you. If Patrick had not asked me to speak about what happened to me as a child I would never have spoken about it. It would have remained a secret deeply hidden that I would take to my grave. I felt really sad that my boy had inherited something so terrible from me; but talking to him now I know that he has moved away from being damaged by it.

> He passed on to me the draft of your book. I will not tell you it was an easy read, for it was not. I put it down many times, and shed many tears; moved especially by the story of Elsa which made me want to tear down that community and any church building I could find. I still rage at how something supposed to be so benevolent should in fact be so malevolent and corrupted.
>
> I have, however, realised that for me the burden has lifted. I cannot change the past, but I am living in the future; mostly without flashbacks, intrusive memories or anything of the sort. I did go for some counselling as you suggested, but have not really found it necessary. I also have a so much better relationship with Patrick, and my wife. We have started going away and living a lot. That feels really good.

The stories it seems go on; new narratives start to take the place of the original trauma saturated ones. The research and conversations are now out of my hands and beyond the remit of this book. Email conversations fire between various contributors, copying me in, but the stories have moved on without me. Liz suggests a suitable ending:

> "Laughing and talking with friends
> casts the past away.
> Files it;
> not in a locked drawer
> but in a slot marked 'history'".

BIBLIOGRAPHY

Abarbanel, A. 2012. From secular to sacred, from despair to hope: a therapist's spiritual journey. *BACP Thresholds* Autumn:14-19.

Abraham, N., and M. Torok. 1994. *The shell and the kernel: renewals of psychoanalysis volume 1 Trans. Rand, N.T.* Chicago: University of Chicago Press.

Afana, A.H., D. Pedersen, H Ronsbo, and L.J. Kirmayer. 2010. Endurance is to be shown at the first blow: social representations and reactions to traumatic experiences in the Gaza Strip. *Traumatology* 16 (4):73-84.

Alexander, P.C. 1992. Application of attachment theory to the study of sexual abuse. *Journal of consulting and clinical psychology* 60:185-195.

Ashworth, J., and I. Farthing. 2007. Churchgoing in the UK: A research report from Tearfund on church attendance in the UK. Teddington Middlesex: Tearfund.

Atkinson, J. 2002. *Trauma trails: Recreating songlines: the transgenerational effects of trauma in indigenous Australia*. North Melbourne: Spinefex Press.

Belsky, J., and J. Cassidy. 1994. Attachment theory and practice. In *Development through life: a handbook for clinicians*, edited by M. Rutter and D. e. Hay. Oxford: Blackwell Science.

Bender, L., and A. Blau. 1937. The reaction of children to sexual relations with adults. *American Journal of Orthopsychiatry* 7:500-518.

Bonanno, G.A. 2004. Loss, trauma, and human resilience: have we underestimated the human capacity to thrive after extremely aversive events? *American Psychologist* 59 (1):20-28.

Bond, T. 2000. *Standards and ethics for counselling*. London: Sage publications.

—. 2004. *Ethical guidelines for researching counselling and psychotherapy*. Rugby: British Association of Counselling and Psychotherapy.

Bowlby, J. 1944. Forty four juvenile thieves: their character and home lives. *International Journal of Psycho-analysis* 25:19-52.

—. 1951. *Maternal care and mental health, World Health Organisation Monograph (Serial 2)*. Geneva: WHO.

—. 1988. *A secure base: clinical applications of attachment theory*. London: Routledge.

Bracken, P.J., J.E. Giller, and D. Summerfield. 1995. Psychological responses to war and atrocitiy: The limitations of current concepts. *Social Science and Medicine* 40 (8):1073-1082.

Brown, A, and D Finkelhor. 1986. Impact of child sexual abuse: a review of the research. *Psychological Bulletin* 99 (1):66-77.

Browne, A, and D Finkelhor. 1986. Impact of child sexual abuse a review of the research. *Psychological bulletin* 99 (1):66-77.

Buzawa, E.S., and C.G Buzawa. 2002. *Domestic Violence: the criminal justice response*. Thousand Oaks: Sage Publications.

Chesterton, G.K. 1996. *The complete Father Brown stories*. London: Wordsworth Editions Ltd.

Church of England. *Review of Child Protection Cases: A House of Bishop's Protocol.* http://www.churchofengland.org/media/36119/cpreviewrtf.rtf 2007 [cited 2012.

—. *Independent child protection survey across dioceses.* http://www.churchofengland.org/media-centre/news/2010/02/pr2610.aspx 2010 [cited 01.07.2012.

—. *Protecting all God's Children: The policy of protecting children in the Church of England 4th Edition* 2010 [cited 1.7.2012.

Clandinin, DJ, and FM Connelly. 2000. *Narrative Inquiry*. San Fransisco: Jossey-Bass.

Cloitre, M., N.A. Morin, and L.O. Linares. 2004. Children's resilience in the face of trauma. *New York Child Study Centre Newsletter* 8 (3):1-6.

Dale, S. 2009. The Grilling of Mr B: Using the narrative therapy practice of 'externalising' conversations to co-research the experience of blindness. *Therapy Today September 2009* 20 (7).

—. 2010. *Where angels fear to tread: having conversations about suicide in a counselling context*. Newcastle upon Tyne: Cambridge Scholars Publishing.

—. 2011. *Songs at Twilight:: a narrative exploration of living with a visual impairment and the effect this has on claims to identity*. Newcastle upon Tyne: Cambridge Scholars Publishers.

Daly, R.J. 1983. Samuel Pepys and post-traumatic stress disorder. *British Journal of Psychiatry* 143:64-68.

Das, V. 2007. *Life and words: Violence and the descent into the ordinary*. Berkeley: University of California Press.

Davies, B. 2000. The Concept of Agency. In *A body of writing*, edited by B. Davies. Walnut Creek,: Alta Mira.

Davies, B, J Browne, E Honan, C Laws, B Mueller-Rockstroh, and E Bendix Peterson. 2004. The ambivalent practices of reflexivity. *Qualitative Inquiry* 10 (3) 360-389.

Davies, B, and S Gannon. 2006. The practices of collective biography. In *Doing collective biography*, edited by B. Davies and S. Gannon. Buckingham: Open University Press.

Davies, B, S Gannon, S Laws, C Rocco, H Taguchi, and H McCann. 2001. Becoming Schoolgirls: the ambivalent process of subjectification. *Gender and Education* 13 (2) 167-182.

Dekel, R., and H. Goldblatt. 2008. Is there intergenerational transmission of trauma? the case of combat vetran's children. *American Journal of Orthopsychiatry* 78 (3):281-289.

Disch, E., and N Avery. 2001. Sex in the consulting room, the examining room and the sacristy: survivors of sexual abuse by professionals. *American Journal of Orthopsychiatry* 71 (2):204-217.

Duba, U. 1995. *Tales from the child of the enemy*. New York: Penguin.

Dube, S., R.F. Anda, C.L. Whitfield, D.W. Brown, V. Felitti, M. Dong, and W.H. Giles. 2005. Long-Term Consequences of Childhood Sexual Abuse by Gender of Victim. *American Journal of Preventive Medicine* 28 (5):430-458.

Dutton, D.G., and T.L. Nichols. 2006. Corrigendum to 'the gender paradigm in domestic violence research and theory: Part 1- the conflict of theory and data. *Aggression and Violent Behaviour* 11 (6):664.

Edleson, J.L. 1999. Children's witnessing of adult domestic violence. *Journal of Interpersonal Violence* 14 (8):839-870.

Ehrensaft, M.K., P. Cohen, Joceyn. Brown, E. Smailes, H. Chen, and J. G. Johnson. 2003. Intergenerational transmission of partner violence: A 20-year prospective study. *Journal of Consulting and Clinical Psychology* 71 (4):741-753.

Ehrensaft, M.K., P. Cohen, J. Brown, E. Smailes, E. Chen, J. Henian, and G. Jeffrey. 2003. Intergenerational transmission of partner violence: a 20-year prospective study. *Journal of Consulting and Clinical Psychology* 71 (4):741-753.

Epston, D. 2004. From empathy to ethnography: the origin of therapeutic co research. *The International Journal of Narrative Therapy and Community Work* 2.

Etherington, K. 2000. *Narrative approaches to working with adult male survivors of child sexual abuse*. London: Jessica Kingsley publishers.

—. 2001. Research with ex-client's a celebration and extension of the therapeutic process. *British Journal of Guidance and Counselling* 29 (1).

—. 2008. *Trauma, drug misuse and transforming identities: a life story approach*. London: Jessica Kingsley Publishers.

Etherington, K (ed). 2003. *Trauma, the body and transformation*. London: Jessica Kingsley Publishers Ltd.

Fater, K., and A Mullaney. 2000. The lived experience of adult male survivors who allege childhood sexual abuse by cliergy. *Issues in Mental Health Nursing* 21 (3):281-295.

Felitti, V., R.F. Anda, D. Nordenberg, D.F. Williamson, A.M. Spitz, V. Edwards, M. Koss, and J.S. Marks. 1998. Relationship of Childhood Abuse and Household Dysfunction to Many of the Leading Causes of Death in Adults: The Adverse Childhood Experiences (ACE) Study. *American Journal of Preventive Medicine* 14 (4):245-248.

Foucault, M. 1980. *Power/knowledge: selected interviews and other writings*. New York: Panthean books.

—. 1997. Friendship as a way of life. In *Ethics Subjectivity and Truth* edited by P. Rabinow. New York: New York Press.

Freedman, J, and G Combs. 1996. *Narrative Therapy: the social construction of preferred realities*. New York: W.W. Norton Company Inc.

French, S, J Swain, D Atkinson, and M Moore. 2007. An oral history of the education of visually impaired people: telling stories for inclusive futures. Lampeter: Edwin Mellen Press.

Fussell, P. 1983. *Siegried Sassoon's long journey*. New York: Oxford University Press.

Gardener, F. 1999. Transgenerational processes and the trauma of sexual abuse. *European Journal of Psychotherapy and Counselling* 2 (3):297-308.

Goodson, Ivor and Sykes, Pat. 2001. *Life History Research in Educational Settings: learning from lives*. Edited by P. Sykes, *doing qualitative research in educational settings*. Buckingham: Open University Press.

Greenwald, E., and H. Leitenberg. 1990. Post traumatic stress disorder in a nonclinical and nonstudent sample of adult women sexually abused as children. *Journal of Interpersonal Violence* 5 (2):217-228.

Harris, T.A. 1995. *I'm ok, you're ok*. London: Arrow Boods.

Haug, F (and others). 1987. *Female sexualization: A collective work of memory* Edited by T. b. E. Carter. London: Verso.

Helzer, J.E., M.D. Lee, N. Robins, L. McEvoy, M.A.N. Engl, and J. Med. 1987. Post-traumatic stress disorder in the general population. *The New England Journal of Medicine* 317:1630-1634.

Herman, J.L. 1992. *Trauma and Recovery*. New York: Basic Books.

Holt, S., H. Buckley, and S. Whelan. 2008. The impact of exposure to domestic violence on children and young people: a review of the literature. *Child Abuse and Neglect* 32 (8):797-810.

Howe, D, M Brandon, D Hinings, and G Schofield. 1999. *Attachment theory, child maltreatment and family support*. Basingstoke: Macmillan press.

Institute of Health and Welfare, Australian, and Australian Centre for Posttraumatic Mental Health. *PTSD Review - Prevalence, prediction and psychological treatment* http://ww.acpmh.unimelb.edu.au/research/ptsdReview.html 2004 [cited 25.11.11.

Itzin, C. 2006. Tackling the health and mental health effects of domestic and sexual violence and abuse, edited by DH: Department of Health and National Institute for Mental Health Home Office London.

Jacobs, M. 1998. *The presenting past: the core of psychodynamic counselling and therapy second edition*. Buckingham: Open University Press.

Jenkins, P. 2002. *Legal issues in counselling and psychotherapy*. Edited by T. Bond, *Ethics in practice*. London: Sage.

Josselson, R, A Lieblich, and D P McAdams. 2003. *Up close and personal: the teaching and learning of narrative research*. Washington: American psychological association.

Kardiner, A, and H Spiegel. 1947. *War, stress and neurotic illness (revised edition) The traumatic neuroses of war)*. New York: Hoeber.

Kendall-Tackett, A. 2000. Physiological correlates of childhood abuse: chronic hyperarousal in PTSD, depression and irritable bowel syndrome. *Child Abuse and Neglect* 24 (6):799-810.

Kitzmann, K.M., N.K. Gaylord, A.R Holt, and E.D Kenny. 2003. Child wintesses to domestic violence: a meta-analytic review. *Journal of Consulting and Clinical Psychology* 71 (2):339-352.

Kolbo, J.R., E.H. Blakely, and D. Englemann. 1996. Children who witness domestic violence: a review of empirical literature. *Journal of Interpersonal Violence* 11 (2):281-293.

Leiner, B. 2009. The Legacy of War: An Intergenerational Perspective (this article not subject to US copyright laws). *Smith College Studies in Social Work* 79 (3-4).

Levendosky, A.A., A.C Huth-Bocks, M.A. Semel, and D.L. Shapiro. 2002. Trauma symptoms in preschool-age children exposed to domestic violence. *Journal of Interpersonal Violence* 17 (2):150-164.

McCloskey, L.A., and J.A. Bailey. 2000. The Intergenerational transmission of risk for child sexual abuse. *Journal of Interpersonal Violence* 15 (10):1019-1035.

McLaughlin, B.R. 1994. Devastated spirituality: The impact of clergy sexual abuse on the survivor's relationship with god and the church. *Sexual Addiction & Compulsivity: The Journal of Treatment & Prevention* 1 (2):145-158.

Meares, R. 2000. *Intimacy and alienation: memory, trauma and personal being*. London: Routledge.

Merrick, M. *Child Abuse and the Church*. http://michaeltmerrick.wordpress.com/2011/07/30/child-abuse-and-the-church/ 2011 [cited 01.07.2012.

Milchman, M S. 2003. 'Implicit memory' cannot explain dissociated traumatic memory: a theoretical critique. *Journal of Trauma and Dissociation* 4 issue 1.

MIND. 28.10.11. *Post traumatic stress disorder*. www.mind.org.uk/help/diagnoses_and_conditions/post-traumatic_stress_ disorder 2011 [cited 28.10.11].

Morgan, A. 2000. *What is narrative therapy? An easy to read introduction*. Adelaide: Dulwich Centre Publications.

Mower, O. 1962. Freud and theory of personality. *The Journal of Nervous and Mental Disease* 135 (4):378.

Mullen, P.E., J.L. Martin, J.C. Anderson, S.E. Romans, and G.P. Herbison. 1993. Childhood sexual abuse and mental health in adult life. *The British Journal of Psychiatry* 163:721-732.

Myerhoff, B. 1979. *Number our days*. London. New York: Meridian published by Penguin group.

—. 1982. Life history among the elderly: Performance, visibility and remembering. In *A crack in the mirror: reflexive perspectives in anthropology*, edited by J. Ruby. Philadelphia: University of Pennsylvania.

—. 1986. Life not death in Venice: It's second life. In *The anthropology of experience*, edited by V. Turner and E. Bruner. Chicago: University of Illinois Press.

Noll, J.G., P.K. Trickett, and F.W. Putman. 2003. A prospective investigation of the impact of childhood sexual abuse on the development of sexuality. . *Journal of Consulting and Clinical Psychology* 7 (3):575-586.

O'Brian, K. 2004. The intergenerational transference of post traumatic stress disorder amongst children and grandchildren of Vietnam veterans in Australia: An argument for a genetic origin. Review of current literature. Paper read at Centre of Social Change Research at Queensland University of Technology, Australia.

Onyx, J, and J Small. 2001. Memory Work: the method. *Qualitative Inquiry* 7 (6) 733-786.

Parker-Hall, S. 2009. *Anger, rage and relationship*. Hove: Routledge.
Payne, M. 2000. *Narrative therapy*. London: Sage Publications.
Pelzier, D. 2002. *My story*. London: Orion Media.
Powell, A. 2012. Open Heart open mind: conversing with the soul. *BACP Thresholds* (Summer):10-15.
Putman, F.W. 2002. Ten-year research update review: childhood sexual abuse. *Journal of American Academy of Child and Adolescent Psychiatry* 41 (3):269-278.
—. 2003. Ten-year research update review: child sexual abuse. *Journal of the American Academy of Child and Adolescent Psychiatry* 42 (3):269-278.
Ravandal, E., G. Lauritzen, O. Frank, and I. Jansson. 2001. Childhood maltreatment among Norwegian drug users in treatment. *International Journal of Social Welfare* 10:142-147.
Reichel, S. 1989. *What did you do in the war daddy?* New York: Hill and Wang.
Resnick, H.S., D.G. Kilpatrick, B.S. Dansky, B.E. Saunders, and C.L. Best. 1993. Prevalence of civilian truama and posttraumatic stress disorder in a representative national sample of women. *Journal of Consulting and Clinical Psychology* 61 (6):984-991.
Richardson, L. 1990. *Writing strategies; reaching diverse audiences*. California: Sage publications.
Richardson, L. 2003. Poetic representation of interviews In *Postmodern Interviewing*, edited by J. Gubrium and J. Holstein. London: Sage.
Rodriguez, N., S W. Ryan, H. Vande Kemp, and D. W. Foy. 1997. Posttraumatic stress disorder in adult female survivors of child sexual abuse: A comparison study. *Journal of Consulting and Clinical Psychology,* 65 (1):53-59.
Rohsenow, D.J., R. Corbett, and D Devine. 1988. Molested as children: a hidden contribution to substance abuse? *Journal of Substance Abuse Treatments* 5:13-18.
Rosenheck, R. 1986. Impact of posttraumatic stress disorder of World War II on the next generation. *Journal of nervous and mental disease* 174 (6):319-327.
Rothschild, B. 2000. *The body remembers: the psychophysiology of trauma and trauma treatment*. London: W.W. Norton.
Rutgers. 2012. Rutgers Oral History Archive http://oralhistory.rutgers.edu/.
Salter, A.C. 1995. *Transforming Trauma: A guide to understanding and treating adult survivors of child sexual abuse*. California: Sage Publications Ltd.
Scauben, L.J., and P.A. Frazier. 1995. Vicarious Trauma: The effects on female counsellors of working with sexual violence survivors. *Psychology of Women Quarterly* 19 (1):49-64.
Schwab, G. 2010. *Haunting legacies: violent histories and transgenerational trauma*. New York: Columbia University Press.
Segman, R., R. Cooper-Kazaz, F. Macciardi, T. Golster, Y. Halfon, T. Dotroborski, and A Shavelev. 2002. Identification of the first gene in posttraumatic stress disorder. *Molecular Psychiatry* 7:903-907.
Sinason, V, ed. 2002. *Attachment trauma and multiplicity: Working with dissociative identity disorder*. Hove: Brunner-Routledge.

Skodol, A.E. 2010. The Resilient Personality. In *Handbook of Adult Resilience*, edited by J. W. Reich, A. J. Zautra and J. Stuart-Hall. London: The Guilford Press.
Speedy, J. 2004. Living a more peopled life: definitional ceremony as inquiry into therapy outcomes. *International Journal of Narrative Therapy and Community Work* 3:43-53.
—. 2005. Collective biography practices: collective writing with the unassuming geeks group. *Briish Journal of Psychotherapy Integration* 2 (2):29-38.
—. 2005. Using poetic documents: an exploration of poststructuralist ideas and poetic practices in narrative therapy. *British Journal of Guidance and Counselling* 33 (3).
—. 2006. Collective Biography Workshop, at Bristol University.
—. 2007. *Narrative Inquiry and Psychotherapy*. Houndsmill: Palgrave Macmillan.
Stearns, J. K. 2011. *Dancing in the glory of monsters: the collapse of the Congo and the great war of Africa*. New York: Public Affairs, a member of the Perseus Books group.
Stith, S.M., K.H. Rossen, K.A. Middleton, A.L. Busch, K. Lundeberg, and R.P. Carlton. 2004. The intergeneration transmission of spouse abuse: a meta-analysis. *Journal of Marriage and Family* 62 (3):640-654.
Strachey, J, ed. 1953-1976. *The standard edition of the complete psychological works of Sigmund Freud*. London: Hogarth.
Swinton, J. 2001. *Spirituality and Mental Health Care: Rediscovering a 'forgotten' dimension*. London: Jessica Kingsley Publishers.
Tedlock, D. 1983. *The spoken word and the work of interpretation*. Philadelphia: University of Pensylvania.
Terkel, S. 1997. *The Good War: An Oral History of World War II* New York: New Press.
Terr, L. 1991. Childhood traumas: an outline and overview. *American Journal of Psychiatry* 148 (1):10-20.
Virag, T. 1984. Children of the holocaust and their children's children: Working through current trauma in the psychotherapeutic process. *Dynamic Psychotherapy* 2 (1):47-61.
Wales, Catholic Bishops' Conference of England and. 2007. The Cumberlege Commission Report:: Safeguarding with confidence: Keeping children and vulnerable adults safe in the Catholic Church. London: Incorporated Catholic Truth Society.
White, M. 1995. *Re-Authoring Lives*. Adelaide: Dulwich Centre.
—. 2000. Reflecting teamwork as definitional ceremony re-visited. In *Reflections on narrative practice: essays and interviews*, edited by M. White. Adelaide: Dulwich Publications.
—. 2003. Definitional ceremony and outsider witness responses. In *narrative therapy and community work conference*. Adelaide: Dulwich Centre http://www.dulwichcentre.com.au accessed 30.5.07.
—. 2007. *Maps of narrative practice*. London: W.W. Norton and Company Ltd.
—. 2007. Working with trauma. Paper read at International Conference of Narrative Therapy and Community Work, at Norway.

White, M , and D Epston. 1990. *Narrative means to therapeutic ends*. New York: W.W. Norton and company.

Whitfield, C.L. 1995. *Memory and abuse: remembering and healing the effects of trauma*. Deerfield Beach, CA: Health Communications.

Winter, D., S. Bradshaw, F. Bunn, and D. Wellsted. 2009. Counselling and psychotherapy for the prevention of suicide: a systematic review of the evidence. Lutterworth: British Association of Counselling and Psychotherapy (BACP)

Wolfe, D.A, C.V. Crooks, V. Lee, A Mc Intyre-Smith, and G. Jaffe. 2003. The effects of childrens exposure to domestic violence: a meta analysis and critique. *Clinical child and family psychology review* 6 (3):171-187.

Yehuda, R., S.M. Engel, S.R. Brand, and J Seckl. 2005. Transgenerational effects of posttraumatic stress. *Clinical Endocrinology and Metabolism* 90 (7):4115-4118.

Yehuda, R., S.L. Halligan, and R. Grossman. 2001. Childhood trauma and risk for PTSD: Relationship to intergenerational effects of trauma, parental PTSD, and cortisol excretion. *Development and Psychopathology* 13 (3):733-753.

INDEX